Miracles That I Have Seen

Miracles That I Have Seen

by

William Arthur Ward

Unless otherwise indicated, all scripture references are from the Authorized King James Version of the Bible.

McDougal Publishing is a ministry of
The McDougal Foundation, Inc., a Maryland nonprofit
corporation dedicated to spreading the Gospel of
the Lord Jesus Christ to as many people as possible
in the shortest time possible.

Published by:

McDougal Publishing
P.O. Box 3595
Hagerstown, MD 21742-3595

ISBN 1-884369-79-0

Printed in the Unites States of America
For Worldwide Distribution

Contents

Foreword by Ruth Heflin ....
Introduction ....

1. Speaking Miracles into Existence 1
2. God Has a Key for Every One of the Six Locks 4
3. My Son Hears of Two Women Healed of Cancer 5
4. I Hear Years Later of a Blind Man's Healing .. 6
5. My Wife Anoints a Dead Magnolia Tree 8
6. My Wife Commands a Truck to Stop 9
7. My Son Bill Prays for His Dog 10
8. Three Ladies Came from California to Texas 11
9. My Miracle Trip to South America 12
10. Thirty Thousand Dollars in the Afternoon Mail 18
11. A Gun is Pointed at Me, but the Man is Saved 21
12. The Ambulance Beats Me to Church 23
13. A Boy is Saved in San Quentin Penitentiary. 24
14. My Left Leg is Almost Cut Off with an Axe .. 25
15. Running on a Badly Sprained Ankle 26
16. Entering Russia in 1972 28
17. Kicking Poverty Out the Door 29
18. A Healing in China 30

19. Out of Gas, But Not Out of Power 30
20. A Giant for God Is Saved through a Tract 32
21. Preaching to Cows 34
22. Admiral Byrd at the North and South Poles. 34
23. A Lady Healed When I Was a Boy 35
24. My Broken Arm Is Healed 36
25. A Doctor Speaks of the Healing of My Arm . 40
26. I Had to Hitchhike Home.............................. 42
27. Receiving $30,540.00 in One Week.............. 44
28. I Had Nickel Faith 49
29. I Graduated to Five-Dollar Faith 50
30. I Graduated to Ten-Dollar Faith.................... 51
31. I Graduated to Hundred-Dollar Faith........... 52
32. I Graduated to Thousand-Dollar Faith 56
33. Today, God Adds to My Money...................... 57
34. You Should Have Ever-Increasing Faith........ 58
35. Tex Sawyers Gets a Volvo.............................. 58
36. A Boy Gets a New Backbone in Bogota, Colombia 60
37. Delivered by an Angel 61
38. God Sends Nineteen Dollars to Our House . 63
39. The Deacon Who Would Not "Deak" 65
40. A Miracle Happened As I Was Going out the Door 68
41. God Paid for a Six-Hundred-Mile Trip 70
42. The Potato Story.. 73
43. My Sister Put the Children on the Porch...... 75
44. The Bill Was Paid Out of a Rat's Nest 76
45. A Nosebleed That Helped Get a Boy Saved . 77
46. They Came to Kill One Another, but God ... 79
47. Love Conquers All 80

48. A Champion Is Made 83
49. An Unexpected Ten Dollars 84
50. He Acted Just Like an Angel, Anyway 84
51. The Wife of the Chief Justice of the Supreme Court 86
52. "You Have Disgraced the Clergy Today" 87
53. A Cool Breeze Blows in the Desert................ 88
54. I Am Able to Preach 89
55. Just About Everyone Was Telling Me How to Die 90
56. Let Me Spend My Last Night on Earth in Church... 92
57. Cross-Eyes Straightened 93
58. The Night That I Was Hit with a Slight Stroke 94
59. The Woman a Hundred Thousand People Called 'Mother' 94
60. There Is a Whole Case of the Milk in the Attic 95
61. Miracles Under Wigglesworth 97
62. A Wigglesworth Meeting.............................. 98
63. He Meant to Slit My Throat from Ear to Ear 99
64. The Vision of Winning Children for God .. 101
65. Jack Coe Could Not Get into His Own Revival 102
66. The President of Phillips Petroleum........... 103
67. "It Is in the Top Drawer in the Dresser" 104
68. "With That Kind of Faith You Will Walk Today"... 105

69. The Steering Wheel Came Off in His Hands 106
70. Sobered Up, Saved and Healed of a Broken Back 107
71. "We Are Going to Chase You Out of Town" 108
72. Receiving a Tent on a Mountain 111
73. "Before Eleven O'Clock in the Morning" ... 115
74. An Angel Rode in the Car with Me 116
75. Thirty Ten-Dollar Bills 117
76. Meeting a Friend at the Garden Tomb in Jerusalem 119
77. God Directs Our Paths 120
78. A Young Man Was Struck by a Golf Ball 121
79. My Revival on a Greyhound Bus 121
80. "I Don't Ever Want to See Your Face Again" 124
81. "You Will Receive a Nasty Letter Every Day" 125
82. Knowing Things by the Holy Ghost 127
83. A Boy Comes Home 128
84. "Look At That Piece of Junk He Is Driving" 129
85. God Can Heal Broken Elevators 130
86. A New Car, the First Thing in the Morning 132
87. A Man Was Going to Commit Suicide in Las Vegas 133
88. My Son Was Kneeling on the Ball 134
89. Finding Where I Was Staying in Rome, Italy 135
90. Three Doctors Could Not Find Her Gall Bladder 136
91. A Thousand Dollars Came in the Mail 138
92. The Second Mortgage is Paid 139

93. Bob Hope Told Sid Solomon to Get My Book 141
94. "That Lady Who Was Paralyzed is Healed". 142
95. A Paralyzed Woman Healed Over Period of Months 143
96. God Uses a Man from the Insane Asylum... 143
97. New York City Miracles 145
98. God Works at Both Ends of the Tent 147
99. I Am Afraid of Dignified People 148
100. "You Will Be Blind in About Six Months"... 149
101. My Wife Gets a New Automobile 150
102. I Get a Three-layer Chocolate Cake 152
103. Receiving a New, Four-Bedroom Brick Home 153
104. He Did Not Need the Special Shoe Any Longer 153
105. God Healed My Broken Automobile 154
106. Three Hundred Dollars Was Given to Me in Jerusalem 155
107. About to Go over the Falls in a Canoe 156
108. Saved from a Watery Death in the Chesapeake Bay 156
109. "Doctor, He Does Not Have Heart Trouble" 158
110. "Flying Upside Down, Holding on for Life" 159
111. A Man Is Brought from Kentucky to Arizona 160
112. "Come Home Immediately; Bobby Has Polio" 161

113. The Lepers Are Healed in the Bahamas 162
114. "I Broke That Wild Horse" 164
115. The River That Makes Glad 166
116. My Tonsils Were Not Cut, Burned, or Pulled Out 167
117. Staying in the Home of Rev. R. L. Scarbrough 169
118. Miracles with Children 170
119. A Lady Is Healed of Polio 170
120. Deafness Was Healed Instantly 171
121. Oral Roberts' Tent Was Given to Rex Humbard 172
122. I Was Baptized in the Holy Spirit 173
123. My Mother Saw the King and Queen of England 176
124. Singing in Front of the White House 178
125. Put Twenty Dollars Worth of Gas in the Car 180
126. My Son Billy Swallowed a Pendant 180
127. She Is Brain-dead and Does Not Know Anything 181
128. The Church Building in Richmond Is Bought 182
129. The Orson Welles Radio Program Hoax 184
130. My Mother Really Was Dying 186
131. Six Hundred Dollars Blew Out of His Pocket 187
132. A Man from India Finds Me in Virginia 188
133. A House Trailer Is Unhurt in Rocky Mount, North Carolina 189
134. I Could Not Leave the City 191

135. A Blind Man Was Healed After We Left the Room 192
136. Please Pray Your Very Best Prayer 193
137. It Is No Use To Pray for That Man 195
138. World Evangelist Called in Ice Cream Parlor 197
139. Healings in Longview, Washington 198
140. I Dreamed of My Niece's Death 199
141. My Aunt Lost Her Voice for Twenty-five Years 200
142. An Eighty-Mile-an-Hour Wind Quieted 201
143. "I Saw One Hundred and Fifty-three People Lying on the Ground" 203
144. They Gave Me a New Packard Automobile 205
145. A Boy, Hit by a Tent Pole, Was Thought to be Killed 206
146. The Perfume of Her Desire Followed Her . 208
147. Woman Who Did Not Want to Come to the Tent 209
148. Sixty-three Doctors Said It Was Impossible. 211
149. The Preacher Said, "God Does Not Heal Today" 212
150. God Calls As a Man Is About to Commit Suicide 213
151. Two Water-head Babies in Texas 214
152. There Is Over $1,300 Cash in This Building 215
153. A Demon-possessed Woman Tried to Choke Me 217
154. "How Many Revivals Have You Held?" 218
155. Three Short Straws 220

156. Three Thousand Dollars, A Thousand at a Time 222
157. Existing in a Totally Dark Room 224
158. I Received a Strange, Wonderful Letter 226
159. "Put Your Husband's Shoes Under Your Bed" 227
160. Walking Against the Traffic 228
161. A Man Lay in a Coma Twenty-Eight Days 228
162. I Have Never Been Out of My House in Nine Years 229
163. The Prophetic Gift 229
164. A Tankful of Blessing 230
165. The Wheel Bounced Right over My Car 231
166. Mother, You Are So Much Taller 231
167. In the Name of Jesus, I Create 232
168. I Missed the Number by One 233
169. I Missed the Number by Two 234
170. $50,000 and $300,000 235
171. Christmas When I Was A Boy 236
172. Following in a Great Man's Footsteps 239
173. You, Too, Can Have Miracles 241

Foreword by Ruth Heflin

I know of no one who has experienced more miracles than Uncle Bill, Mother's brother. He has not only experienced them for himself, but he has believed and declared them for countless numbers of people across this country and around the world. In fact, when people think of Dr. Ward, they think of miracles.

Uncle Bill and Mother grew up in a household where miracles were the order of the day, as normal as breath itself. Life with their mother, Sophia Evans Ward, was a life full of miracles. And both he and Mother have carried on that life of miracles they had learned at grandmother's feet.

Last February on Uncle Bill's birthday, I sat at the table in our camp dining room with him and another great man of God. Having heard my uncle recount miracle stories since my childhood, I have a number of favorite ones, and I began to draw from his deep well of miracles by asking him to tell my friend some of those stories. I asked him again about the miracles pertaining to his altar calls, about several particular miracles pertaining to money, about miracles of healing, and even about the miracle of God revealing to him the names and addresses of people who were opposing his revivals.

As he regaled us with story after story that day, we seemed to relive them with him. It was a spiritual banquet that challenged us all to believe God for greater miracles for our own lives and ministries.

I am so happy now that many of the great miracles he remembers will now be enjoyed by people around the world through this book, *Miracles That I Have Seen.*

Introduction

I was born February 11, 1916, in Abingdon, Virginia, just as the whistles were heralding the fact that it was twelve o'clock noon. Before I was a year old, our family moved to Washington, D.C., where we lived about five blocks from the White House.

When I was about five years old, Evangelist William E. Booth-Clibborn from England was conducting a revival in our church. He was, I think, the grandson of William Booth, who founded the Salvation Army. One night in the middle of his sermon, the evangelist left the platform and came down to me. He placed his hands on my head and exclaimed, "God shows me that this boy is going to become a great preacher some day and preach all over the world." He then returned to the platform and finished his sermon. I knew that he was telling the truth, because that day my mother had told me the same thing, and I was feeling the call of destiny.

Dr. William A. Ward
Richmond, Virginia

-1-

Speaking Miracles into Existence

I went into Cincinnati, Ohio, to hold a revival meeting. When I got into town, I saw advertisements concerning my meetings, which read, "Come hear a man who speaks miracles into existence." I became upset, and said, "I never said that I can speak miracles into existence." I went to my room feeling low in my spirit.

In my prayer hour, God told me to get a pen and paper and write down every miracle that I could remember that happened in my revival meetings. I believe that I wrote down more than two hundred miracles. Then God showed me that, in a sense, I had spoken every one of them into existence, for speaking the word of faith is a part of producing the miracle. After a fashion, you get what you say. Nobody can get a miracle talking doubt and unbelief. "Maybe" and "Perhaps" never created a miracle. You speak the word in faith, and God brings it to pass in victory. Hallelujah! After God showed me this truth, I went into that revival with renewed vigor and redoubled energy.

So, God showed me that I have a miracle in my mouth, and instead of praying so much about the problem, I could prophesy to the problem in faith. I felt so good about this revelation, which was new to me, that I went to church determined to use it.

At the church they were having people call in twenty-four hours a day for prayer. They were calling in from all over America. The next morning, I walked into the auditorium just as the telephone rang. I asked a lady at the telephone if I could answer the phone, for God had spoken to me about speaking miracles into existence.

When I picked up the phone, a lady was crying. She was calling from Minneapolis. She cried, "They just operated on my brother in the hospital here in Minneapolis, and they found that his brain is filled with cancer. They sewed his head up and declared, 'There is nothing we can do for him. He can only live a matter of weeks.' Please pray for him."

I answered, "Sister, your brother is healed of cancer right now while I am talking to you. I want you to have the doctors examine his brain again, and they will find no cancer. They will pronounce him cured and dismiss him from the hospital, and he will be in our revival here in Cincinnati next Sunday morning."

You know, I forgot all about that phone call, but the next Sunday morning when I went into the auditorium, a very excited woman came to me, saying, "Brother Ward, I am the woman who called you from Minneapolis about my brother who had cancer of the brain. It happened exactly like you told me. I called back to the hospital; they examined my brother's brain again; and they could find no cancer.

They pronounced him cured, and he is in this church service this morning. He wants to meet you."

I followed her. Her brother jumped up and cried, "I am healed by the power of God, and I have brought eight of my relatives with me today to be saved."

Brother W.V. Grant, Jr. was the pastor of the church. When he came into the service, the special gift of God which he has began to operate, and he told those eight people their names and addresses, and other things. All eight of them were converted. Thank God.

Now, I could have prayed the woman's problem over the telephone, saying, "Dear Lord, this woman's brother has cancer of the brain. He is in the hospital in Minneapolis. He needs healing." God already knew all of that. Instead of praying the problem, I prophesied the solution. In my heart, I knew that God wanted to heal him and that God was looking for someone to stand in the gap and exercise faith for the man. I determined to be that person who would have faith for the fellow's healing. So I prophesied by faith, and God did the healing. We can only work with God. He needs us to believe, and we need Him to work the miracle.

From that time until now, I have prophesied miracles into existence knowingly. Before that, I prophesied miracles into being by exercising faith in God and speaking out that faith, but perhaps not really understanding what I was doing. Of course, I have always known that God is the miracle worker, and we give all of the glory to Him.

Oh, my brother, speaking the word in faith is one of the greatest things that you can do. Amen! I said, "In faith." Praise God! In the next three weeks, I saw about fifty miracles take place through my speaking them into existence. You have to believe that God is in the revivals with you. You are not there operating under your own power. You are there as a representative of God, and God says, "Speak the word, and I will bring it to pass." Of course, I must again state that I am no healer. I could not heal anyone. We people who pray for the sick only claim to be God's servants. God is the healer, and He alone.

- 2 -

God Has a Key for Every One of the Six Locks

I was conducting a revival meeting in Fayetteville, North Carolina. One night, Brother and Sister Coons, who were working with me in the campaign, came to me at the altar. She was crying as though her heart would break. She said, "Brother Ward, our daughter who is only sixteen got on drugs. Her mind is gone. They have put her in a mental hospital in California. They have her behind six locked doors, and they will not let us see her. Please pray for her."

I could have prayed the problem, which God

knew all about anyway, but I did not. Instead faith leaped into my heart, and I began to prophesy the solution. I said, "God has a key for every one of those six locks. He goes into that hospital and heals your daughter right now. Her mind is restored to her. The doctors will reexamine her, pronounce her cured, and release her from the hospital. They will put her on an airplane, and she will be here in Fayetteville, North Carolina, next Sunday. She will be saved, and God will fill her with the Holy Ghost."

Rev. and Mrs. Coons later told me that it all happened exactly as I had prophesied.

- 3 -

My Son Hears of Two Women Healed of Cancer

God told me one time, "You speak the word in faith, and I will bring it to pass." Many times we speak the word in faith, but we never hear about the results, because we have to travel to the next town. But I have learned a long time ago to leave the results in God's hands. For I cannot heal anyone, but I can believe. And I am sure that if I do my part God will do His part.

My oldest son is an Assembly of God minister. He went into North Carolina to conduct a revival meeting. When he returned home, he phoned me, all excited, "Dad, I am going to tell you something that you probably don't know. The minister in the church, where I have been these last few days, told me that twenty-five years ago he asked you to hold him a revival. You said, 'I can only come Sunday morning as I am scheduled in other churches.'

"He told me that he had two ladies in his church who were in the hospital dying with cancer. He went to the hospital, got the two ladies and brought them to the Sunday morning meeting to have you pray for them. You prayed over each one of them, saying they would be totally healed. That has been twenty-five years ago. The women are still healed, still living and attending his church."

I shouted over the phone, saying, "I never heard about that, but God is so good to let me hear of things like this even many years later to let me know that He has heard me. I am His and He is mine. I dedicated my life to serve Him, and these reports are the rejoicings of my life."

- 4 -

I Hear Years Later of a Blind Man's Healing

Then I told my son of another healing that I had just heard of after twenty-five years. I had conducted a tent revival in Carlsbad, New Mexico. In front of my hotel, a blind man sold newspapers and magazines at a stand. Every day when I would buy my paper, I would talk to him about the meetings I was conducting and ask him to attend them. I would say, "If you come and let us pray for you, God will heal you."

I never remembered that he ever came to the meetings, but twenty-five years later, when I was preaching in the Full Gospel Business Men's Convention in West Texas, a lady came to me and declared, "Wasn't that wonderful about that blind man being healed in Carlsbad, New Mexico?"

I replied, "What blind man was that?"

She answered, "I heard you preach in Carlsbad, and there was a blind man who sold newspapers and magazines in front of your hotel. He used to have a sign on the stand that said, 'I am blind and selling papers for a living.' He came to the service on the last night of your tent meeting. God healed him, and he put up a sign, 'God healed me of blindness, and I am closing my stand.' For twenty-five years he has gone all over town telling people how God healed him. I still live in Carlsbad, and I see him all the time. He is the greatest witness for Christ that I know in Carlsbad. Wasn't that a wonderful healing?"

I replied, "Yes, but I hadn't heard of it before. I will never forget that man, for I witnessed to him every time that I would buy my daily paper."

- 5 -

My Wife Anoints a Dead Magnolia Tree

It has been such a joy to me to see how my family believes God just as I do. One day about four years ago, I heard my wife praying. I saw her get a bottle of olive oil and march out of the house. By her look and her determined walk I knew that something was on her mind. I watched out of the window.

Now, we had gone through a terrible winter, and the snow and ice had killed a magnolia tree that we had on the side of our house. I saw my wife go up to the dead tree and anoint it with oil. I quietly raised the window so I could hear what she was saying. She cried, "I command this tree to live in the name of Jesus." Then she said, "Tree, you are going to live again in the name of Jesus." She came back into the house and did not even mention to me what she had done.

I wish that you could come by our house and look at that tree. It is alive, flourishing, and such a blessing to us. I praise God each time that I see it.

I have testified about that tree so much that the old devil got angry, and the other day he tried to destroy it. We had a large tree near it with a huge dead branch on it. That great dead branch broke off and began falling toward the magnolia tree. I cried to the Lord and, at the last second, God caused that dead limb to veer, and it just knocked off one small piece of the magnolia. I have been thanking God for His protection ever since. He is mindful of even small things that affect our lives.

- 6 -

My Wife Commands a Truck to Stop

I told you that every miracle that I tell reminds me of another miracle, so I just remembered another miracle where my wife was involved. Our son Elvin had just been married, and we needed to move tables and chairs from the church to another auditorium where the reception was going to take place.

My wife and I came down the church steps, and she was telling me that we had to hire a truck to move the things. Just then, she saw a truck coming down the street about a block away. She cried, "Dear Lord, that is exactly the kind of truck I need and the kind of man I need to help move this furniture. I command that truck to stop and help us in the name of Jesus."

Suddenly, that truck pulled over and stopped right in front of my wife. She asked the truck driver, "Why did you stop right here?"

He said, "I don't know, I just suddenly decided to stop and look in that store window across the street."

My wife answered, "I will tell you why you stopped, because I prayed to God to have you stop. We need help. How much will you charge us to move some tables and chairs to the auditorium up the street?"

He replied, "Nothing, I don't want any money, I

just want to help." He jumped out of the truck and gladly helped load it.

My wife said, "Look how strong he is. He picks up those long tables like they are nothing." I was thankful for how quickly God answered my wife's prayer. God is a part of our existence. He is so precious and cares about every detail of our lives.

- 7 -

My Son Bill Prays for His Dog

While I am talking about my wife, let me tell you about an incident with my youngest son. He was twenty years old, and one day he came running in the house, gasping, "Dad, come quickly! My dog is having a fit."

I ran outside with my son, and the dog was foaming at the mouth. His legs were so wobbly that he could not stand up, and he kept falling on the ground. My son started for the dog, and I screamed at him, "Stay away! The dog might have hydrophobia, and you could get rabies."

But my son did not listen to me. He went over, put his hand on the dog's head, and cried, "Devil, take your hands off my dog. This is my dog. He does not belong to you. If you want a dog, you get your own dog, but you leave my dog alone." Then he talked to God, and said, "Dear Lord, I command my dog to be healed right now, in the name of Jesus."

I know that it was not my faith, because I was worried about my son. It was my son's faith, and the dog immediately was healed. He quit foaming at the mouth. His legs became strong again, and he had no more seizures.

It makes me so happy to see all the members of my family exercising faith and believing God for miracles, when they are necessary.

- 8 -

Three Ladies Came from California to Texas

Two preachers and I were traveling to Dallas to attend a convention. About thirty miles before we came to the city, we stopped at a Stuckey's restaurant to get a bite to eat. We walked by three black sisters who were eating in the restaurant. God dropped a revelation in my soul. I stopped and said, "You three ladies are not from Texas."

They said, "That's right!"

I continued, "You live in Los Angeles, California. In fact, you go to Dr. Frederick G. Price's church."

They shouted, "That's right!"

"You three are all saved, and you have been filled with the Holy Ghost."

They again said, "That's right!"

"And the reason that you are in Texas is because you (I pointed to the oldest woman) have cancer, and you asked these two ladies to drive with you. You have come to Texas to get a preacher to pray that you will be healed of the cancer."

They shouted, "That's right!"

I said, "Well, I am a preacher; I am in Texas; I believe in healing; and God told me to pray for you to be healed." I prayed right out loud in that restaurant, because I believe that if people can curse in front of me in public places, I can pray in front of them.

I wish that I could tell you that I know that God healed that woman, but I never saw her before nor since. I have never heard from her. I have no proof that God healed her, but I operate on the principle that God wanted to heal her, and He gave me a revelation of her need. He laid a burden upon me to pray the prayer of faith for her; and if I did my part, I have to believe that God did His part. He is the Healer. I believe that He performed His healing work.

It is so much easier to believe when you can base your faith upon a revelation that God gives you.

- 9 -

My Miracle Trip to South America

I had a great burden to go to South America and conduct revival meetings, but I did not have the money to go. I prayed all week that God would send me, but I am ashamed to say that I talked badly to the Lord on this occasion.

I said, "Dear Lord, if You don't send me to South America, then take that scripture out of the Bible which says that the fields are white unto harvest but the laborers are few. For I am offering my services as a laborer, and You would be refusing my services." Now, I know that was the wrong way to pray, but I was desperate. I had been fasting and praying all week. I had a tremendous burden upon me, and sometimes we don't think clearly under those circumstances. At any rate, I have repented for the way that I talked to God.

In my defense, I might say that husbands and wives who live together, love each other, and talk closely with one another, sometimes talk badly to each other and have to ask for forgiveness. That is the way I felt. God and I were living together, loving one another, and talking closely with each other. And yet I had overstepped myself in my prayers. Isn't it wonderful that God can put up with us and our shortcomings. He is so patient. I sometimes think, "Dear God, You could have wiped us off the face of the Earth, but You did not, and You still love us. Glory to Your Name."

After praying all week to go to South America, but telling no one but God about my desires, I went to the church in Richmond. As I stood behind the pulpit to preach, my niece, Rev. Ruth Heflin, who was pastoring in Jerusalem but happened to be home, came up behind me, placed her hand on my head, and said, "Thus saith the Lord, 'Thy feet shall stand on foreign soil within one week.' " I accepted that prophecy, saying, "I receive that in the name of Jesus."

I might say before going on: if you expect a prophecy to come true, you should believe it, take it, and cooperate with it. I can prophesy that you will receive a great blessing from the Lord, but if you do not believe it, and go around saying, "I don't believe that, I will never get a great blessing," don't worry; you probably will not get it. Then you will proclaim that I am a false prophet, but I will counter with the thought that you are a false believer. You would not believe, and "Without faith it is impossible to please God." So God may not give His prophetic gifts to those with whom He is not pleased.

I would tell you what I would do, if someone prophesied that I was going to get a great blessing, I would accept it and cooperate with it. I would be LOOKING for the blessing. I would turn my faith loose, TESTIFYING that I was getting a great blessing, and I would be EXPECTING it to come soon.

I know that this is the long way round to my point, but you see, I want to teach a little as well as tell about miracles. In that way some of you may be benefited to receive miracles, also.

When my niece prophesied that I would stand on foreign soil within one week, I did not have to ask, "What foreign soil?" for I had been praying to go to South America. I knew foreign soil, at this time, did not mean Africa or China. God was letting me know that He was answering my prayer. I immediately called the airlines about tickets for South America; I packed my suitcases; and I began telling people that I was going to South America.

When it came time for the last plane to leave Richmond that could connect with another plane leaving Florida, that would get me on foreign soil within one week, I was flat broke – which was not that unusual. But I took my suitcases to the airport in Richmond. I did not even have the change to use the pay phone and call home to say another good-bye. I waited in the airport. When there was only fifteen minutes left before the plane would leave, my sister, Rev. Edith W. Heflin, came into the airport. She said, "Oh, I was afraid that you might have left. I have brought you something." She handed me a white envelope. I quickly opened the envelope, and there was $300 in it.

I went over and bought my ticket, which was $298 and checked my bags. Just before I got on the plane, my sister prophesied over me that I would not only go to Bogota, Colombia, but that I would preach in nine different countries in South America, going from the north to the south. As she said "Nine different countries," I was fingering the $2 I had in my pocket. I thought: "Nine countries on $2 ... This will be a great miracle." And indeed it was. For, as she prophesied, I preached in nine different countries from the north to the south in South America.

May I digress again to explain why I constantly advise people not to try something because it worked for me. A man said, "Brother Ward went to the airport with no money, and God sent him the money to go to South America at the last minute, so He will do the same for me." The man wanted to go to a certain country and with no money, so he packed his bags, went to the airport, telling everybody that God would send him the money at the last minute. But the money never came in, and he had to return home in defeat. He and others were embarrassed. He perhaps did not have my revelation. Furthermore, he possibly had not fasted, prayed, and agonized before God all week until the revelation came.

Moreover, I have seen people wonderfully healed by the power of God, while other people who had the very same affliction and said, "God is no respecter of persons, if He healed that person He will heal me, too," were not healed – at least at that time. I don't have the full answer, but perhaps they did not pay the same price in consecration. They did not have the same faith, or they had not gone all the way with God in obedience.

Let me continue the story of my trip to South America. When I reached Miami, Florida, where I had to change planes for Bogota, Colombia, it was after 11:00 P.M. By the time that I got my suitcases and reached the counter of the airlines, it was midnight. The plane for Colombia did not leave until three o'clock in the morning. I told the man behind the counter that I wanted to be on that plane. He really laughed and said, "You and hundreds of others. I have been standing here for hours telling people that the plane is full, and we have a waiting list of hundreds more. There is no way that you can get on that plane."

Since my niece had prophesied over me that my feet would stand on foreign soil within one week, I knew that the 3 A.M. plane was the last plane that could carry me so that I would be on foreign soil within a week. I knew that I would be on that plane. I told the attendant that I would be on the plane, and he laughed again. He said, "I have a waiting list of people who are ahead of you that is longer than my arm. I guarantee that you will not be on that plane."

I continued to stand there at the counter for three hours, exercising my faith. "Thank You Jesus, You told me that my feet would stand on foreign soil within one week. I know that I will be on that plane. Your word is true. It never fails."

People were coming by and checking their baggage with the attendant. Five or six times he asked me, "Why don't you go get a motel room and get some sleep?" He would also tell others who were waiting, "You might as well get a motel room and get a good night's sleep. I tell you that all the seats are taken on this plane." Finally, he sold the last ticket to someone who was on his list. He turned to me and gleefully said, "You see, I told you so. I just sold the last ticket. The plane is full. Go home."

Then it was just like someone had slapped him in the face. He snapped around and said to the man who had gotten the last ticket, "Do you have a ticket out of Colombia?"

The man answered, "No, I don't want to come out of Colombia. I just want to go into Colombia."

The ticket seller said, "I am sorry, but the law says that I cannot sell a ticket to you, unless you have a ticket out of Colombia. Give me that ticket back." When he had the ticket back, the attendant started down his list that was longer than his arm. Loudly he called name after name. Evidently they had all gone to get their motel rooms.

Exasperated, he finally turned to me, and said, "What a miracle! You are really going to be on that plane after all." He shouted over to another attendant, "I have just seen the greatest miracle. This guy would not leave the counter, and he kept telling me he was going to be on this plane, and he is."

I asked the ticket seller, "Would you like to see the card that I have been holding in my hand for the three hours that I have been standing here?"

He said, "Yes, what is it?" I showed it to him. It was a card that Oral Roberts had sent me, and it read, "EXPECT A MIRACLE."

If you don't expect something good to happen, it probably will not. But if you get your faith and expectancy working full tilt for you, good things are going to happen, for God has a miracle for you.

- 10 -

Thirty Thousand Dollars in the Afternoon Mail

Sister Chan phoned me in Richmond from the Bronx, New York. She was crying, "I was supposed to receive a letter with thirty thousand dollars in it several weeks ago. It is either lost or someone may have stolen it. Please pray that the letter will be found."

I answered her, "Sister Chan, don't you worry another minute. You will receive the thirty thousand dollars in the afternoon mail today. Call me back and tell me about it."

She called back, saying, "Thank God, Brother Ward, the money did come in the afternoon mail, just as you said it would."

You can call it coincidence, if you want to, but after you have seen hundreds of instances where you spoke the miracle into existence, and it happened exactly as God led you to say it, it makes a believer out of you.

In regard to this story of the thirty thousand dollars coming in the afternoon mail, you may say, "That money had to be mailed before you ever prayed." That does not bother me at all. For I operate on that scripture that says, "Before you call I will answer." Because of His foreknowledge, God knows that a child of His is going to speak the word in faith, and He starts the ball rolling ahead of time, so to speak. You know that God is not limited by time. He answers before the fact or after the fact. It is just that someone has to pay for the miracle with the currency of Heaven, which is faith.

Sister Chan told her friend Sister Adams about my speaking the miracle into existence. So Sister Adams, also of the Bronx, New York called me. She was upset, she said, "Brother Ward, they have arrested my youngest son. The judge is going to try my boy tomorrow. Everyone says that they are going to make an example of my son, and throw the book at him. I don't want him to go to jail. Please pray."

I answered her, "Sister Adams, they may have thrown the book at your son, but since you have called on God, He is going to turn everything around. The judge will be extra lenient on your son tomorrow. Everyone will be astonished as the judge lets your boy off free. Call me back and tell me about it."

She phoned me back, and reported, "Brother Ward it happened just as you said, the judge let my son off free."

I have people say to me, "I would speak things into existence, but I am afraid that they will not come to pass." I answer, "Then you are full of fear, and fear and faith cannot exist in the same heart at the same time. Get rid of fear, and have faith in God."

God told me, "You speak the word in faith, and I will bring it to pass, as long as it is a righteous cause. You represent me. I send you out to work for me. I am backing you up in everything that you do, provided it is a holy cause."

God is just as interested in my speaking the truth as I am. He does not want one of His children going around speaking untruths. I feel that He is just as much obligated to me as I am obligated to Him. I am obligated to live right and to exercise faith in my

Lord. He is obligated to do His part in working the miracle, for I am just an errand boy.

I cannot work miracles, yet I believe in miracles, and I have enough sense to know that miracles are in Christ's department. He worked them while He was on earth, and He is still working them. And we are obligated to give Him all of the glory for the miracles. This we will gladly do. We give all of the glory to our lovely Lord. He is the only true miracle worker. Hallelujah!

- 11 -

A Gun is Pointed at Me, but the Man is Saved

More than thirty-five years ago, I was on my way to preach in a service at our church in Richmond, Virginia. I stopped in a drugstore. A man, who said that he was "six feet, ten inches tall, barefooted," was sitting at a table drinking from a bottle of whiskey. He shouted, "Hey bud, come over here and drink whiskey with me."

I answered, "I don't drink." He took out a long pistol, laid it on the table, pointed in my direction, and said, "When I ask a man to drink with me, he either drinks with me or suffers the consequences."

I could see that he had three guns on him: a gambler's gun up his sleeve, one in his belt and one, which he had just laid on the table. I went over to him, put my hand on his shoulder, and smiled, "You won't shoot me. I am a preacher and God is with me. I am on my way to church. I am going to pray for you, and you will come to my church, 2701 Hull Street one night and be converted. You will be delivered from this liquor and will never drink again."

That man (his name is Leslie Creed) came one night and was converted. His two brothers, his sister, his brother-in-law, and other relatives were all converted. I preached his father's funeral, and my sister preached his mother's funeral.

Leslie Creed told me the other day, "When I got saved, you were having meetings in the church every night in the year, and I never missed a service for three and a half years, although I had to hitchhike thirty-five miles each way to church." Mr. Creed has never forgotten the date of his conversion. He tells everyone, "I was saved on August 14, 1957, and I have never had a drink since."

For years, Mr. Creed was my right hand man at the church, helping me with the work. I saw him carry the front end of a large, upright piano down three flights of stairs, when three or four men were carrying the back end. He was a giant of a man, but when God got a hold of him, He really got a hold of him.

Just the other day, a doctor told Leslie, "I prescribe four ounces of liquor for you every day. It will open the arteries that go to your heart."

Brother Creed said, "Doctor, the Lord delivered me from liquor over thirty-five years ago. I have not had a drop of the stuff since, and if it takes that to cure me of blood cholesterol, I'll keep the cholesterol."

- 12 -

The Ambulance Beats Me to Church

Back in 1947, I was conducting a revival meeting in Taft, California. One night, just before church service, I was asked to go to the hospital and pray for a woman who was dying of cancer. When I finished praying for her, I said, "I will see you in church." I left the hospital and drove back to the church.

When I entered the auditorium, I saw the woman that I had just prayed for in the hospital. She was standing on the platform singing. She saw me come in and ran back to me shouting, "I am healed! I am healed!"

I answered, "Lady, I left you in the hospital and drove straight to church. How in the world did you get to the church before I did?"

She laughed, "When you left, I knew that I was healed. You said, 'I will see you in church,' so I told the doctor that I was coming to church."

He replied, "Well, we will send you in an ambulance."

- 13 -

A Boy Is Saved in San Quentin Penitentiary

I spoke to two thousand people nightly for five weeks in San Francisco, California, in 1940. The warden of San Quentin Penitentiary asked me to pray with a twenty-year-old boy, who was going to be the first man in the history of California to die in the gas chamber. California had used hanging for executions, but was changing to the gas chamber.

The man told me that he was going to die in two days because his mother had given up on him. She was a pseudo-phrenologist. She felt that she could read the bumps on a person's head. The boy told me that he had heard his mother tell people many times, "Feel this bump on my boy's head. He will commit murder some day." He stated, "I felt that if my own mother doesn't have any confidence in me, what's the use?"

He continued, "I surrendered to evil, became a criminal and did commit murder." Then he added, "Preacher, see that little room across the hall? I am going in there day after tomorrow and die, but it's because my mother gave up on me."

I asked him to kneel and pray with me. He prayed the sinner's prayer, and I believe that he was truly converted. He was ready to meet the Lord when he went into the "little room across the hall." Even if your mother gives up on you, you can still make Heaven.

God has made it so easy for you to get saved. The most unnecessary thing in all the world is for a sinner to die and miss Heaven, because Jesus died on the windswept summit of Golgotha's brow for your salvation. Then the Lord put twelve gates in the New Jerusalem to show you that He can provide an abundant entrance into Heaven for you, no matter what the circumstances are. So just ask Jesus to forgive you for every sin, and He assuredly will.

- 14 -

My Left Leg Is Almost Cut Off with an Axe

In Washington, D.C., when I was nine years old, I cut my left leg with an axe. I cut through veins, arteries, and around the bone. This happened at two o'clock in the afternoon and, at the same time, God appeared to my mother in the Woodward & Lothrup Department Store in downtown Washington, where she worked, and said, "Your son has just cut his leg with an axe; if you do not pray, he will bleed to death." My mother went into a room where the women try on their new dresses; she stayed in there praying for me until she knew that she had the victory.

I thought that my mother would be so shocked

when she came home and saw my leg. I felt that she would surely faint, but she was not a bit surprised; she knew all about it. God had revealed it to her, and she had prayed through. The first words that she spoke when she entered the front door were these, "How is your leg, son?"

I answered, "It is all right."

Although the axe had severed veins and arteries, mother found only three drops of blood at the scene of the accident. Mother fasted and prayed nine days and nights for me. At the end of that time, my leg was perfectly healed, and I went out and played with the other boys. I never had a stitch taken in my leg. If it had not been for prayer, my leg probably would have been amputated. But because of prayer, I have never had any trouble with that leg, and I played college baseball, basketball and football.

- 15 -

Running on a Badly Sprained Ankle

In 1940, when I was twenty-four years old, I was conducting a revival meeting in Ottumwa, Iowa. Early in the first week I went into Des Moines and played basketball. I leaped in the air and came down on the side of another fellow's foot, spraining my left ankle badly.

When I returned to Ottumwa, I could not bear to

put the left foot on the floor. Imagine my embarrassment when I had to hop on one foot into a packed-out church that night, where people were waiting to hear me preach. I had to stand on one foot to preach, holding the pulpit for support. Toward the end of my sermon, the power of God came on me, and I ran around the entire church and jumped up and down on both legs in total victory. But after church, when the power of God had lifted, I had to hop out of the church on one leg.

The next night, the same thing happened. I hopped into the church on one leg. Toward the end of my sermon, the power of God came on me, and I again ran completely around the church. The third night, the same thing occurred. I had to hop into the church on one leg, and toward the end of my sermon, the power of God came upon me and I ran around the church again, jumping up and down on both legs. But again, after the power lifted, I had to hop out of the church on one leg. I saw that the power certainly was not of me. It was the supernatural power of God, and when it was upon me, I had absolutely no pain, but when it lifted, I was only human, and in great pain again.

I had a wonderful revival in Ottumwa, preaching every night for five weeks. Many souls were saved and many people were healed.

- 16 -

Entering Russia in 1972

In 1972, I first went to Russia as a member of a tour group, which Dr. Wallace H. Heflin, my nephew, was conducting. As we entered the country, passing through customs, our luggage was searched. Under the old Communistic regime, they searched for Bibles and tape recorders. They confiscated the Bibles and tape recorders of all in the group, but when they came to my luggage, I prayed, "Dear Lord, don't let them see my Bible or tape recorder."

The man searching my suitcase had his hand on my Bible, when his superior yelled at him, "Get his Bible and tape recorder."

He answered, "I have been looking, but he does not have a Bible or tape recorder." Consequently, of the fifty-seven people on the tour, mostly preachers, I was the only one who carried his Bible and tape recorder all through Russia.

When we were leaving the country, the authorities said, "We have lost your Bibles and tape recorders; You will have to leave without them. We can't find them anywhere."

My nephew answered, "I am phoning the President of the United States and telling him that you will not give us our Bibles and tape recorders." Within two or three minutes, they suddenly appeared with all Bibles and tape recorders.

- 17 -

Kicking Poverty Out the Door

When I pastored in Richmond and was on the radio three times a day, a man called me to come pray for his wife and himself. He said that he was so poor that they could not pay their bills, and they had nothing to eat. I stood in the living room with them and prayed. While I was praying, the woman walked over and opened the front door. She made so much noise, I opened my eyes to see what was the matter. I saw her give a kick at the open front door. I hurriedly said, "Amen," and asked her what she was doing? She shouted in victory, "I have just kicked poverty out of the door!"

The next day, they brought me $100, saying, "God just sent us a thousand dollars today, and we have brought you the tithe."

The following day, they gave me $50, averring, "God just gave us $500 today, and we are bringing you the tithe."

In a day or two, someone gave them the money to enroll in Bible college, and they soon became preachers. They got on the road to prosperity, when they kicked poverty out of the door.

- 18 -

A Healing In China

One day in China, the Heflin tour group was visiting a large hospital, praying for the sick. As we walked down the corridor, we passed a room. My attention was fastened on a man lying on a bed. He was having acupuncture treatments and seemed to have more than fifty needles protruding from his flesh. I left the tour group, and hurried into the room, placed my hand on the man's head and prayed for him. As I was going out of the room, I heard all of this noise and turned around to see this fellow pulling needles out of his flesh, reaching for a coat, and placing a hat on his head. I asked our tour guide what the man was shouting. He replied, "He is crying, 'I am healed! I am healed, and I am going home!' "

- 19 -

Out of Gas, But Not Out of Power

When my oldest son was only seven years old, he and I left Tulsa, Oklahoma, in the car, headed for Charlotte, North Carolina, to conduct a revival in Garr Auditorium there. We were driving all night, and at two o'clock in the morning we ran out of gas when we were nearing the top of a mountain in western North Carolina. I had been wanting to buy gas for a long time, but we were driving through the mountains, and no gas station was open.

Out of gas, the power steering would not work properly, the power brakes would not function correctly, and we began to go back down the mountain. I could not see behind me, and the road was full of curves. I knew unless God helped us, we would be killed. I prayed, "Dear Lord, I must be the dumbest boy that You have in Your family, but I am still your boy. So I command in the Name of Jesus that this car run, gas or no gas, and take us to the next gas station safely." I put my foot on the starter and the motor came on, purring like a kitten. We went up that mountain and drove about thirty miles up and down mountains, until we finally came to a gas station that was open.

I pulled into the service station and asked the attendant, "Do you mind putting a stick in my gas tank and telling me what you see?"

He put a stick in the tank. I heard it hit the bottom. It came up bone dry.

The attendant said, "You could not have gone another foot."

I replied, "If your gas station was twenty or thirty miles up the road, and it was the only one open, I would have been able to run until I reached it, because I was running on the power of God, not motor fuel." I then witnessed to him how I had come about thirty miles on empty.

I continually ask people not to try to do things because I have done them. You may get in trouble, because you may not have the same conditions that I had. God had work for me to do, and He knew that my foolishness would have gotten my son and me both killed. My son, John Robert Ward is a preacher, just as I am. The Lord wanted to use the two of us. Furthermore, you know that I would never, under any circumstances, deliberately try to operate an automobile on empty. It would never work.

- 20 -

A Giant for God Is Saved through a Tract

My mother and sister taught me to hand out tracts. When we would ride the streetcar or bus, I knew that everyone on board would get a tract. When we would walk to church, I knew that everyone who met us would receive a tract. As a boy, nine years of age, I used to stand in front of our church before the services began and hand out tracts to the passers-by.

One day I was in Oral Robert's office in Tulsa, Oklahoma, when I was thirty-five years old. Oral Roberts said, "Brother Ward, I want you to meet Dr. Myron D. Sackett. He is the head of all my work in Europe and in the Holy Land. He is a great man of God, and I love him." He continued, "Dr. Sackett, I want you to meet William A. Ward."

Dr. Sackett began to ask me questions, "Did you use to live in Washington, D.C.? Did you attend

Brother Collier's church, when it was at 930 Pennsylvania Avenue in Washington? Did you use to hand out tracts to people as they walked by the church when you were just nine years old?"

I answered, "Yes" to all of his questions.

He grabbed my hand and said, "You are responsible for my salvation. You handed me a tract. I went down to the corner and read the tract under the light of the street lamp. I came back and asked you your name, and how old you were. You said, 'William A. Ward.' I never forgot your name. You said, 'Service is just about to start, why don't you go upstairs and attend the meeting?' I did, and I was converted. I met your mother and your sister. Thank you for handing me that tract." I left Oral Robert's office, walking in the wonder and glory of God.

About two years ago, my sister felt that she should go from the Arctic to the Antarctic, giving out tracts. She did; she handed out tracts through Alaska and on down into Tierra Del Fuego on the southern tip of South America. She handed out tracks just two hundred miles from the South Pole.

My sister's large purse is always full of tracts. I have been with her, giving out tracts in China, Africa, and many other nations. So you see, the ministry of handing out tracts that our mother taught us when we were children, has been with us through a lifetime.

- 21 -

Preaching to Cows

As a boy, I dreamed of being a preacher. I preached to my sister's dolls. When I went to the country, I would preach to the hogs or to the cows. I will never forget one time when I was about twelve years of age, I was preaching to the cows on a farm in West Virginia. Far in the back of about two hundred cows, there was one stubborn cow in the pasture. I pictured her as a sinner, and I said to myself, "I am going to do my best to get that sinner to the altar." I kept pleading for that stubborn cow to come to the altar in front, and I have never forgotten how that cow began to wind her way through all those other cows. She came up front to the fence and put her nose right up to my hand. I felt just as if I had gotten that cow to the altar. And if they have cows in Heaven, I know that cow will be one of them.

- 22 -

Admiral Byrd at the North and South Poles

When I was eleven or twelve years of age, there was a man in our church in Washington, D.C., whose name was Hughson. He was the chief steward on the Admiral Byrd ship, and when he was getting ready to go to the North Pole with Byrd, he told me, "Admiral Byrd will drop a United States Flag at the Pole."

I said, "I wish that Admiral Byrd would drop a Bible and our wonderful church magazine, *The Pentecostal Evangel,* when he drops the flag." Mr. Hughson told Admiral Byrd that a boy wanted him to drop the Bible and magazine, when he dropped the flag.

So when Admiral Byrd went to the North Pole, he dropped three things: a United States flag, a Bible and *The Pentecostal Evangel.* Then when the Admiral went to the South Pole, he also dropped a United States flag, a Bible and *The Pentecostal Evangel.* So this message of Pentecost has gone around the world. You may look from the North Pole to the South Pole, and you will find the message of Pentecost there.

- 23 -

A Lady Healed When I Was a Boy

Also, when I was eleven or twelve years old, a lady in our church, named Mrs. Deere, asked my mother to have me come and pray for her. She said, "I have been sick for many years. I have traveled all over America seeking healing. I've gone to Dr. Charles S. Price's meetings, Brother Wigglesworth's revivals, Sister McPherson, and all of the great evangelists and prayer warriors who believe in healing. But I have not been healed. However, last night, I had a strange dream.

In my dream, the Lord spoke to me, saying, 'The trouble has been that you have had faith in people, rather than God. You have traveled three thousand miles to have one preacher pray for you and hundreds of miles to have others pray for you, and your faith has been in the person, not in God. Now, you know that young boy, William Ward. You have known him all of his life. You know that he does not have healing power. You call him, and have him pray for you, and you will be healed, because you will not have faith in him, but you will have faith in God.' "

"So," she averred, "I want young William to pray for me." She was blind, she was deaf, she had rheumatism, heart trouble, and I don't know how many other afflictions. God instantly healed her when I went over to pray for her; she was perfectly delivered of all her problems, got out of bed, and went back to church, where she loved to testify about her experience. She enjoyed relating how she had gotten her faith in God and not in instrumentalities.

- 24-

My Broken Arm Is Healed

At age seventeen I was preaching, but as I received no money for preaching, I painted houses in order to pay my bills. I was painting this house in Washington, D.C., and I had the hiccups. I don't know what caused me to say such a foolish thing, but I said, "Dear God, You have healed me of a lot of things in my life, but now if You can heal me of these hiccups, then I will trust You the rest of my life. I will know that if You can heal a little thing like hiccups, then You can heal any bigger thing. If You heal me of these hiccups today, then You can allow anything to happen to me tomorrow, and I will trust You for it." I did not hiccup another time, and I was instantly healed.

The next day I was painting above a second-story window, and I had done another very foolish thing. I had my ladder on the cement, and the cement sloped toward the street. The ladder slid out from under me, and I fell more than two stories, landing on the cement. I broke my left arm at the elbow; the bones were protruding about an inch and a half through the flesh. As I looked at my arm, immediately I thought of what I had said the day before, "Dear Lord, if You will heal me of hiccups today, I will trust You for any big thing that happens to me tomorrow, and believe that You can heal it."

Just then the lady of the house, where I was painting, came running out crying, "Lie right there; I have called for an ambulance, and it will be right here."

I said, "I am going home and pray; God will heal me; and I will be back tomorrow to finish painting your house."

She cried, "I thought that you landed on your arm, but you must have landed on your head!"

I said, "Regardless of what I landed on, I'll be back tomorrow and finish painting the house." And I was.

I arrived home at three o'clock in the afternoon. The lady where I was staying, asked, "What are you doing home so early?"

I kept my arm covered and answered, "I have come home to pray." I went up to my room, closed the door, and prayed for God to heal me. At six o'clock in the evening I heard the man of the house come in downstairs, so I went down. They could see that my arm was swollen twice its size, and they could see the bones protruding at the elbow. The husband cried, "Come on, we are going to the hospital."

I declared, "No, God is going to heal me."

They retorted, "Listen, we believe in healing, but if God does not heal you, gangrene may set in, and they may have to amputate your arm. Then people will blame us because it happened while you were at our house."

I said, "Nobody is going to blame you, because God is going to heal me."

The man shouted, "I guess that I will have to pick you up bodily and carry you to the hospital."

I replied, "No!" I started up the stairs as fast as I could go with him right behind me, and his little thin wife right behind him. When I got in my room, I prayed, "Dear Lord, paralyze him, so that he cannot get a foot over the threshold to get me."

He came right to the doorway, and his wife said, "Go get him."

He answered, "I can't move. I'm paralyzed. I can't get my foot over the threshold."

In my room I began to pray. I said, "Lord, You healed me of hiccups yesterday, You can heal me of a broken arm today." It seemed like a cloud of glory filled my room like the cloud of glory that filled Solomon's temple. Over the left hand corner of my room, I saw a rainbow and instantly the scripture came to me, "There is a rainbow around the throne," and I said, "Bless God, one end of the rainbow is around the Throne of God, and the other end of the rainbow is around my room. My room is connected to the Throne of God."

As I prayed, God spoke to me and said, "Lift your Bible over your head and I will heal you." I picked up the Bible in my right hand and raised it over my head, and God said, "No, lift your Bible in your left hand."

I replied, "Wait a minute, Lord, you know that my left arm is broken, and I can't lift my Bible with my left hand. You know that my left hand is so sore that even if I touch my little finger, I can't stand the pain, and I can't close my fingers over the Bible and lift it up. But I will try. In the name of Jesus, for the glory of God, I am going to lift my Bible over my head with my left hand." Slowly, but surely, I got the Bible over my head, but nothing happened. I was not healed. I cried, "Lord, You said that You would heal me."

The Lord spoke to me, and said, "And yet one more thing will I require of thee, clap your hands and I will heal you."

I cried, "Dear Lord, I can't clap my hands. I can't stand the pain if I just touch my hand. But I will try it in the name of Jesus, for the glory of God." I began to clap my hands slowly and then I increased the tempo until soon I was clapping my hands as hard as I could, and I was shouting, "Glory to God." I heard a snap, and I looked, and the bones had gone in. The pain was entirely gone, and I began to dance up and down in the Spirit of God, saying, "Praise God, I am healed! I am healed!"

While I was shouting, I looked over, and the man of the house had grabbed his little, thin wife, and they were dancing around and around, saying, "Praise God, he's healed! He's healed!" I have never had any trouble with that arm from that day until now.

- 25 -

A Doctor Speaks of the Healing of My Arm

My broken arm was healed in Washington, D.C., when I was seventeen years old. Sixteen years later, when I was pastoring a church in Tulsa, Oklahoma, a Jewish medical doctor that I played volleyball with saw me coming out of Oral Roberts' office in Tulsa. He began walking with me. He said, "I just saw you coming out of Oral Roberts' office. You are not one of those preachers who believe in that healing stuff are you?"

I answered, "I certainly am! Do you see my left

arm? Well, that arm was broken, and two bones were protruding from the flesh near the elbow, and God healed my arm."

He retorted, "I don't believe any such thing as that! I don't believe that your arm was ever broken. You just thought that it was broken." He continued, "My office is not far from here; come to my office and I will x-ray your arm and prove to you that it was never broken."

I answered, "Doctor, first, I want to tell you that my left arm has been broken six times. The doctors fixed it the first three times. They told me that if I ever broke it again they would have to amputate it. I am sure that they were trying to scare me; I was just a boy. They did a good job of it; for I never went back to the doctor, and God has healed it three times."

I went on to say, "My arm was always broken in or around the same place, halfway between my elbow and my wrist. But the healing I was telling you about was when I was painting above a second-story window, and the ladder, which was resting on the cement walk, slipped out from under me. I fell more than two stories, landed on the cement, and broke my left arm. The bones were broken either at or near the elbow, and two bones protruded at the elbow."

The doctor replied, "Here's my office; you come up. I will x-ray your arm and prove to you that no bones were broken at or near the elbow." So we went into his medical office. He x-rayed my left arm in different positions. He examined the x-rays and soon returned, saying, "God, help us! You were entirely right; your arm was broken at the elbow; but it healed perfectly. I have never seen a broken arm mend as well after we have set it." I was so glad that he took the x-rays, because he began telling people all over Tulsa of the miracle.

-26-

I Had to Hitchhike Home

In the summer when I was seventeen years of age and between my first and second years of Bible college, I pastored three churches on a circuit in western Maryland. One Monday morning, I did not have the money to pay my way home to Washington, D.C., which was about two hundred and fifty miles away, so I decided that I would hitchhike. I arose at six o'clock in the morning and began to hitchhike home. The night before, I had preached on the subject, "Keep an Open Heaven," and I told people that no matter what trouble came their way they could keep Heaven open.

When I was out on the highway, about seven in the morning, it began to rain. It poured down all day. I never got one ride from seven in the morning until four in the evening. I walked in the rain. I only had one suit – my best and only suit – and it shrank. The pant legs and the coat sleeves crept up. My suit was being ruined. The great depression was still on, and my suit loss was a real tragedy. But as I walked in the rain that day, I said, "I am going to keep an open Heaven." I shouted and praised God, and I was happy. I walked along the road singing:

"Farther on the way grows brighter
Count your milestones one by one,
Jesus will forsake us never,
It grows brighter farther on."

As I walked down the road, singing that song at the top of my voice, I could hear windows opening. People were looking and listening to this soaking wet specter singing in the rain.

Along about four-thirty in the afternoon, I knelt down beside the road and prayed, "Dear Lord, I have been faithful to You all day long. I preached last night on 'Keep an Open Heaven,' and all this day I have kept Heaven open. I have not griped or grumbled; I have not fretted or fumed. You have seen that I have passed the test with flying colors. I may be soaking wet, muddy, and cold, but I am still your man. Not one car has stopped for me all day long, but I command the next car that comes down the highway to stop and pick me up, and not only take me to Washington, D.C., but right to my front door."

The next car that came down the road stopped, picked me up, and took me to Washington. When we got in town, the driver asked, "Where do you live?" I told him and he said, "I drive within a block or two of your house. I will just drive you home." He took me to my front door. This is one of the ways in which God has taught me many lessons through the years. We have to keep Heaven open in the dark hours, so that God can work for us, and bring us into the sunshine.

- 27 -

Receiving $30,540.00 in One Week

We had to have $30,000 in one week, or we would lose our church building in Richmond, Virginia. My sister, Dr. Edith W. Heflin, came over to a church service and prophesied that the $30,000 would come in so easily that we would never know from where it all came. I have often sat down and tried to think of the sources of that money, and I can only remember how the last money came in on the last day.

God has always worked with me on a last minute basis. I call it "Last minute rescues." I once asked the Lord why He waited until the last minute, when I seemed to be going down in the water of trouble for the third time, saying, "Glub! Glub!" He seemed to tell me that it was the only way that I would give the glory to Him for the victory. Otherwise I would think that it was my knowledge or ability that brought the desired answer. He reminded me of Jonah in the belly of the whale. When Jonah knew that education could not help him, money could not help him, friends could not help him, armies could not help him, he cried, *"Salvation belongeth unto the Lord."* He was ready to give the glory to God for deliverance. Then God could work for him.

So I awoke on the last day, knowing that if we did not have the $30,000 in the bank by closing time, we would lose our building. And we still lacked $2,500 of the amount that we needed. I prayed and God told me that a lady in Fredericksburg, Virginia, would bring me the money (He gave me her name and address). Immediately I began to shout and praise God and jumped in my car and drove the fifty-five miles to her house. God had not said one word to me about driving to her house. But I guess I wanted to help God out. When I knocked on her door, she was not home.

Disappointed, I sat on her front steps, waiting for her to come home. Time passed, and I said, "Dear Lord, I have to have the money in the bank by two o'clock. It is getting late; what shall I do?"

The Lord told me that while I sat on her front steps, waiting for her to come home, she and her two children were sitting in my living room back in Richmond, waiting for me to come home. When God tells you something, it is so clear you know that you know. I had not heard an audible voice. God is Spirit, and He bypasses my ear and talks directly to my spirit. But it is so loud that often I think that I have heard it with my ear.

I jumped in my car and drove back home. When I rushed in my house, the lady and her two sons were sitting in my living room. She said, "Brother Ward, when I woke up this morning, God told me to bring you two thousand five hundred dollars. We have been sitting here waiting on you to get home for a long time."

I answered, "I will tell you all about it when I get back. I only have time to get this money to the bank before it closes."

When I entered the bank, one of the officers of the bank went over and locked the door. I had just made it in before their closing. I took my money into the bank president's office and laid it on his desk. I smiled, "I have the thirty thousand dollars. Please count it."

He counted it, and answered, "But, you don't need thirty thousand; you need thirty thousand, five hundred and forty dollars."

Taken aback, I said, "I never knew about the extra five hundred and forty dollars, and the bank is now closed. We don't want to lose our church building."

Then a voice spoke loud and clear to my spirit, and I turned quickly to the president, and said, "Count it again."

He retorted, "I just counted it," but he began counting it again, and then he laughed, "Oh, Preacher Ward, you were only kidding me. You slipped that other five hundred and forty dollars into the money."

I spoke with a shouting faith oozing out of every muscle of my body, "I did not put any other money in there. God did it. You have just witnessed a miracle."

He counted it again and said, "I guess I have.

There was only thirty thousand dollars the first time that I counted it, but there definitely is thirty thousand, five hundred and forty dollars now."

About ten years went by, and I went into a dry cleaning establishment in Richmond. A man rushed breathlessly into the cleaners behind me. I looked and it was the bank president. He fairly shouted, "Preacher Ward, I saw you come into this cleaners, and I double-parked my car to run in here and tell you that I am saved now."

He continued, "I sold the bank and moved to Florida, but I could never forget the way God multiplied that money for you, when you needed it so desperately. I went to church and got saved. When I saw you come in here, I had to run in and tell you."

Today, my sister and my niece are pastors in that same church building, where my sister prophesied that God would send the money in quickly and easily.

We had all of the ingredients in that case that are necessary for a financial miracle. When people come to me and ask, "Pray that I get money," I ask, "How much money?" If they reply, "Oh, it doesn't matter just as long as it is a lot of money," I usually tell them, "You probably will not get it, because God cannot get the glory. How would you know if God answered prayer? If God sent you ten thousand dollars, you would say, 'No, I wanted a million dollars.' "

Just the other day, a woman came to me and said, "Brother Ward, God never answered your prayer."

I asked, "What prayer was that?"

She replied, "I asked you to pray that I would get a lot of money, and I never got it."

I answered, "Lady, I know that you did get some money."

She replied, "I wanted a lot of money, and I only got a thousand dollars."

I said, "You were very fortunate, I only prayed for you to get five hundred."

To me, $500 was a lot of money, but to her $1,000 did not seem to be very much. That is why when you ask for a lot of money, it is difficult for God to answer that prayer, because whatever amount you receive, it would not satisfy you. If you got $1,000,000, you probably would have wanted $10,000,000.

So, to receive a financial miracle from God you have to be specific:

SPECIFIC AS TO THE AMOUNT OF MONEY YOU NEED
SPECIFIC AS TO THE TIME ELEMENT
SPECIFIC AS TO THE REASON YOU NEED IT

Our $30,540 miracle had all the ingredients necessary for a "know so" miracle. We knew:

THE AMOUNT: We had to have $30,000
THE TIME ELEMENT: We had to have it within one week.
THE REASON: We had to have it in order to save our church building.

When you are specific, you know when you get the answer from God, and God can get the glory.

- 28 -

I Had Nickel Faith

I did not start out having faith for more than $30,000. I remember when I had to have faith for a nickel. It has been quite a few years ago. I was preaching at campmeeting, and I had promised a man to phone him at a certain time. It was a business call and a very important one, too. I was driving in the country, and it was drawing near the time when I must call. I saw a pay phone by the side of the road and stopped to use it. The phone took a nickel to operate it in those days.

I was not broke. In fact, I had a hundred dollar bill in my wallet, but I had to have a nickel to use the phone. My word was at stake; church business was at stake. I began to pray for a nickel, and I put legs to my prayers by starting to look on the ground. I found a nickel on the ground and used the telephone. I told about it in church, and someone said, "I would be ashamed to go around looking on the ground for a nickel; I would rather lift my eyes to the heavens and look for stars." I did not say anything, but I thought, "Even if she had all the stars in the heavens, she still could not use the telephone without a nickel."

THE AMOUNT NEEDED: A nickel
THE TIME ELEMENT: Immediate
THE REASON: To keep a business appointment

- 29 -

I Graduated to Five-Dollar Faith

I had Brother Roach, an eighty-year-old man, helping me paint the church building in Richmond. We stopped for lunch, and we were walking in the alley behind the church when he asked, "Brother Ward, can you let me have five dollars? I have to take some groceries home for the family, they have nothing to eat."

I replied, "Brother Roach, I am terribly sorry, but I am just as broke as you are. However, let us pray, and God will send you five dollars for lunch."

We stopped there in the alley, and I prayed, "Dear Lord, You know that Brother Roach needs five dollars. His wife and children are home with no food, and they need lunch now."

When we opened our eyes, Brother Roach said, "Oh, Brother Ward, you were kidding me. You just dropped a five dollar bill on the ground in front of me."

I looked down and there was a five dollar bill lying at his feet. I said, "Brother Roach, I never had five dollars to put there. I never even saw that bill lying there. God loves you and your family. He wants you to have lunch. He put it there for you." He picked up that $5.00 with a shout of thankfulness and hurried off to get the food.

The ingredients for a special miracle were there:

THE AMOUNT NEEDED: $5.00
THE TIME ELEMENT: Immediate
THE REASON: A hungry family needed lunch

- 30 -

I Graduated to Ten-Dollar Faith

One Sunday morning I went to church in Richmond. I gave my money in the offering. I soon remembered that I was out of gas and needed ten dollars. I prayed, "Father, send me ten dollars, as I do not have enough gas in my car to get to my revival tonight."

After the church service, my sister was standing at the door, shaking hands with people. When I shook hands with her, she put a ten dollar bill in my hand. In my heart I said, "Thank You, Jesus."

I had rented the Masonic Temple Auditorium in town for a revival, and that Sunday night, my sister came over to the auditorium before her church service. She was so apologetic. She said, "Oh, brother, I am so sorry. I am so sorry. Please forgive me. I did not mean to do it."

I wondered what she felt so badly about, so I asked her what she meant. She answered, "This morning, I had a ten dollar bill and a one dollar bill in my hand. God told me to give you ten dollars, so I thought that

I had given you the ten, but after you left, I saw that I still had the ten in my hand, and I must have given you the one dollar bill by mistake. Oh, I am so sorry."

I smiled, "You never gave me a one-dollar bill; you handed me a ten. I am positive because I needed a ten, and I was praying for ten, and after I left church and saw the ten, I have been praising God all day."

She shouted, "Oh, thank God, I have felt bad all day, thinking that I had not given you the ten."

God saw that my sister was sacrificing for me. She really needed the ten herself, but loving her brother, she gave me the ten, and God just turned the one dollar she had left into a ten. So she had a ten dollar bill, and I had a ten dollar bill. My God is able. Praise the Lord!

The ingredients for a lovely miracle were there:

THE AMOUNT NEEDED: $10
THE TIME ELEMENT: Immediate
THE REASON: To get an evangelist to his revival

- 31 -

I Graduated to Hundred-Dollar Faith

I was pastoring the church in Richmond. One morning my wife said to me. "We have absolutely no food in the house, the children are very hungry, and we are broke. What are we going to do?"

The situation was desperate, and I began to pray, "Dear Lord, should I quit preaching and go to work, drawing down a salary like other men? If I am to continue preaching, You are going to have to feed my children. You said in Your Word that if a man does not take care of his family, he is worse than an infidel. Now, I cannot be a preacher and an infidel both. You are going to have to work for me and my family today, or You are going to lose a preacher." I continued to pray, and then I set a time limit.

Now, let me intersperse here. Please do not try to do something because I did it, or because any other person did it, for that matter. If you do, you may get in trouble, for you may not have the same revelation, or be at the same level of desperation. In fact, I probably would never do the same thing again, myself. For this reason, I hesitate to tell some things that have transpired between God and me, because I don't want anyone to think that God always works like that. Be assured that He does not work the same way all of the time, even when He works with the same person.

At any rate, I told God, "Unless you send me one hundred dollars by five o'clock, so that I can feed my family, you have lost a preacher." I was praying out loud; my family could hear me. They knew that I was desperate, for I love to preach. I was born to preach. I am never so happy as when I am preaching. Yet, I was saying, "Unless you send me one hundred dollars by 5:00 P.M., I will never preach again. If you are not going to take care of my family, I cannot preach again."

Now, I certainly am not proud of the way that I prayed. In fact, I am terribly ashamed of the way that I prayed; but sometimes desperate situations call for desperate prayers. And, I might add here, I have never been so desperate in prayer, that God did not hear me. I was not praying one of those little "Pretty Please" prayers; I was agonizing before God. They could have heard me crying out to God a block away. I meant business. My life, my future was on the line. If my God was not able to send me money to feed my family, I needed to find out now. In my heart I knew that God had never failed me, and he was not going to fail me this time.

Along about 4:30 P.M., my wife and three children assembled in the living room, where I was bombarding Heaven. About 4:45 one of my children came to me, crying as though his heart would break, "You are not really going to quit preaching, are you, Daddy?"

"If God does not send me a hundred dollars by 5:00 P.M., I will."

Then my wife and the other two children, one after the other, came over and hugged me, crying, "Daddy, please don't quit preaching."

I could only reply, "If God does not send me one hundred dollars by 5:00 P.M., I will never preach another sermon." We were all crying and praying.

If you think that I was just a money preacher, after more money, you have missed the whole train of thought. My family had sacrificed for years. They had lived in the church building, worn the cast off clothing of other children, and gone hungry many times. No, I was a desperate man going around desperation corner.

My wife said, "It is two minutes to five." Then the children half cried, half screamed, "It is one minute to five." The clock on the mantel began to strike five. There was a knock on the front door. My wife, the three children, and I all ran to open the door. I don't know which one of us got there first. A man whom I had never seen before, stood there surprised to see five people flinging the door open to him on his first knock. He said, "I am looking for Dr. William A. Ward."

I answered, "You have found him."

He continued, "I am from Baltimore, Maryland. I left early this morning and drove a three-hundred-mile round trip to bring you one hundred dollars, but I have not been able to find you. I have looked all over Richmond for you. I am glad that I have finally located you. Here is one hundred dollars for you."

I said, "God would not let you find me until five o'clock, because I was praying for God to send me one hundred dollars by five o'clock, and it seems that He always works for me at the last minute. That way I know that He heard my prayer; He sent the money; and He is always on time."

I reiterate, "Don't you try to operate as I have done, because God may not work the same way with you."

THE AMOUNT NEEDED: $100
THE TIME ELEMENT: By 5:00 P.M.
THE REASON: To feed my family

- 32 -

I Graduated to Thousand-Dollar Faith

I was preaching the Preachers' Convention, a three-day convention which we have every January at the Calvary Pentecostal Campgrounds in Ashland, Virginia. I was the evening speaker. I needed $1,000 in order to pay a bill. They received a love offering for me of $1,000. Brother Heflin had earlier received an offering to help buy the land next to the camp, so that they could build dormitory rooms.

God told me to give my entire $1,000 offering to the camp toward the purchase of the land next door. I gave the money, and the next night, they received another offering for me; and it was exactly $1,000. I found again that it is impossible to outgive God.

The ingredients were there for a beautiful miracle:

THE AMOUNT NEEDED: $1,000
THE TIME ELEMENT: Immediate
THE REASON: To pay a bill

- 33 -
Today, God Adds to My Money

Not too long ago, I discovered that it worked when I told God how much money I had to have, before I had my revival campaigns. I went to Flint, Michigan, in 1991, to conduct a revival for my great friend, Rev. Danny Davis. I prayed, "Dear Lord, I must have two thousand dollars. If that is too much for the church in Michigan to give, then send it quickly from some other source, but I am expecting you to meet my need of two thousand dollars."

After the revival, the church gave me $1,300. When I got in my car to drive home, I prayed, "Father, I thank you for the other seven hundred dollars that I need to make up the two thousand for which I asked." When I got home, the phone rang, and I was asked to preach the afternoon meeting at the camp. They had never given me so much money for preaching the afternoon service, but this time they handed me an offering of exactly $700. And, again, I saw that God is in this work with His children, and He is still in control of things. He had heard my prayer and saw to it that I received the total of $2,000 that I needed.

It is certainly not that we are money hungry. In over sixty years of preaching, we have never stipulated any amount that we must have from any preacher or church. But we are God's servants, and He has promised to meet our needs. So we have learned to trust HIM for the meeting of those needs. We are on His payroll not a church's payroll.

- 34 -

You Should Have Ever-Increasing Faith

When I tell you to be specific with God, I also want to tell you that you should have ever-increasing faith to believe God for bigger and better things. A boy came to me the other day; he had just gotten converted, and he told me that he had faith that God was going to give him a brand new $37,000 Lincoln automobile. I should not have done it, for I may have taken a chance on hurting his faith, but I asked him, "Have you ever trusted God for an inexpensive car yet?" I certainly did not want to harm his faith, but I wanted him to know that ORDINARILY your faith has to grow. Some people have kindergarten faith, some have high school faith, some have university faith, and some have graduate school faith. It may take university faith or graduate school faith to trust God for a new Lincoln automobile.

- 35 -

Tex Sawyers Gets a Volvo

When you are specific, you know when you get the answer from God, and God can get the glory. I was holding a revival for the First Baptist Church in Richlands, Virginia. One night, when I was praying for people, the pastor of the church, Rev. Tex Sawyers, asked me to pray for him to get a car. I asked, "What kind of a car?"

He answered, "Oh, any kind of a car. I am not particular, as long as it runs all right."

I said, "You will never get it."

Surprised, he asked, "Why?" "Because you have to be specific with God, otherwise He cannot get the glory."

I continued, "What kind of car do you want?"

"A Volvo."

"A sedan or what?"

"I want a station wagon."

"What do you want on it?"

"Air conditioning."

"What color?"

"Blue."

I prophesied, "You will have that car within thirty days, and every time that you get in it, you will be happy and thank God, because He gave you exactly what you wanted." He received the car within thirty days, and every time that he has taken me somewhere in that car, he has told me how happy he is with it.

In the beginning God

- 36 -

A Boy Gets a New Backbone In Bogota, Colombia

In Bogota, Colombia, South America, I rented a coliseum, seating ten thousand people, for a revival service. A father was holding his son on his lap. I asked the interpreter to find out why. The father replied that his son had no regular backbone. His backbone was like jelly. He had never been able to sit up or stand or, of course, walk. The father had carried his son many miles to the meeting, seeking healing. I prayed for that boy, and he leaped out of his father's arms, landed in the aisle and took off running.

The power of God came on me. I jumped off the platform and started running behind the boy. Then I heard all of this noise behind me. I looked back, and people were coming up out of wheelchairs and running down the aisle. Other folks were throwing their crutches away and running in victory, healed by the power of God.

Now, of course, I cannot heal anyone, but my God can do anything. He can heal any sickness or any problem.

If you can believe the first four words of the Bible, *"In the beginning, God,"* then you can believe in all of the miracles of the Bible and in miracles today. For if God can create this complex universe and keep it running on schedule, He can certainly work any miracle. If you cannot believe, *"In the beginning, God,"* then you will not believe in any of the miracles in this book.

As for me, my life has been lived in the midst of miracles. My sister says that I may have seen more miracles than any man alive. I certainly do not claim this. I have seen more miracles than some, simply because I have lived longer than they have. As I write this book, I am eighty-one years old. This makes me believe that my sister may have seen more miracles than I have, because she is five years older than I am, and her life has been centered around miracles, also. In fact, she has fed many thousands of people, by faith, for many years.

My sister and I have been people of faith, because we had a great mother, who was one of the first to receive the baptism of the Holy Ghost at Azusa Street in Los Angeles. Our mother lived by faith and taught us to live by faith. Our father was a denominational minister, and our mother was a Pentecostal believer. Thank God we learned faith from our mother. Today, we have no preacher in our family from our father's faith, but we have eighteen preachers in our family from our mother's faith.

- 37 -

Delivered by an Angel

The first miracle that I remember was when I was four years of age. I started to run across the street. An automobile came to a grinding stop, as its wheels beat a protest against the pavement. The car almost hit me; the bumper stopped just short of my body. The driver got out of his car and grabbed me in his arms. He was shaking convulsively in every fiber of his being. He cried, “Where do you live?” I pointed to our house across the street. Still holding me in his arms, he went over and knocked on the door. My mother answered the door.

The man shouted, “You had better keep your boy off the street! I almost killed him. The only thing that saved your boy’s life was that a large, powerful angel stood right in front of my car and held his hand up for me to stop. I did not see your son, but I had to jam on the brakes to keep from hitting the angel. As I came to a dead stop and ran around the car, there was your boy standing where the angel had been. You can thank that angel for saving your boy’s life.”

Tears flowing down her face, my mother held me on her lap and said, “William, just the other day a boy riding his motorcycle was hit by a car right where you were, and now you could have been killed; but God has protected you. You are chosen of God for His service. You belong to God. I dedicated you to Him before you were born. Please promise me that you will never allow a drop of beer, wine, or liquor to touch your lips. Always put God first in everything that you do.” I answered, “I promise.” Through the years I have kept that promise. I have never tasted anything stronger than Coca Cola.

- 38 -

God Sends Nineteen Dollars to Our House

I was eight years old. We were always poor, as far as material possessions were concerned. On this occasion, we did not have the money to pay the rent, which was $38. A man came to our house and declared, "If you do not have the rent money by nine o'clock tomorrow morning, we are going to place your furniture on the street." That night we went to church, and I went to sleep. Mother awoke me about two o'clock in the morning and told me it was time to go home. That is about the time that services ended in those days.

We were crossing Pennsylvania Avenue to catch a streetcar home, for our church was in a rented hall on the second floor of a building, which was next door to the present FBI building in Washington, D.C., when suddenly, I was wide awake, asking, "Mother, do you have any money toward the thirty-eight dollars that we need tomorrow morning?"

As we waited for the streetcar, she replied, "Yes, one lady gave me ten dollars, another woman gave me five dollars, and four women handed me a dollar each. I have nineteen dollars."

Now, we were not beggars. My mother had not told anyone that she needed the money. She did not pray out loud, mentioning her need, as I have heard some folks do. But, we were living for God, working for Him, and that is often the way that God supplies

His peoples's needs. You say, "Why, I thought that God would hand the money from His hand to yours." The Bible avers, "Shall MEN give into your bosom." Thank God that Our Lord has many people who listen to the voice of God, when He says, "Give."

At home we prayed and went to sleep. I was awakened the next morning by hearing my mother shouting and praising God. I cried, "What happened, Mama?"

Mother answered, "When I awoke, the Lord told me to look in the sewing machine drawer. I did, and there was a white envelope with a ten dollar bill, a five dollar bill, and four dollar bills in it. I thought that I had placed the envelope which contained the money in the dresser drawer in my bedroom. I supposed that one of you children had moved the envelope to the machine drawer. But, I decided to look in the dresser drawer anyway, and there I found the white envelope with a ten, a five, and four ones. The nineteen dollars in the machine drawer and the nineteen dollars in the dresser drawer made thirty-eight dollars. Oh, hallelujah! We have the rent money!"

My sister told me, sixty-two years after the miracle, that she remembered resting her hand on the sewing machine and praying, as we prayed for the money just before we went to bed, "Dear Lord, put the money right here." He did, and to this day, we don't know how that money got in our house, but we know that God sent it.

I believe that God knows where there is money

that does not belong to anyone, and He can dispense an angel, saying, "My child needs some money; go take him what he needs." Our God never fails, and He is always on time.

- 39 -

The Deacon Who Would Not "Deak"

I was pastoring a church in Maryland, and I had a deacon that would not "deak." Now, if there is anything worse than a "non-deaking deacon," I don't know what it would be. The fellow declared, "As long as Brother Ward preaches in the church, I will never darken the door again." He had the church about split in half; half of the people thought that he was right and half thought that he was wrong. I was only nineteen, and I put the church absolutely first. Anything that hurt the church had to be wrong.

Two months went by, and his wife called me. She said, "I want you to come and pray for my husband; he is dying."

I answered, "Thank God!"

She remarked, "You misunderstood me; I said that he is dying."

I affirmed, "I did not misunderstand you; I have been praying for something to happen."

She continued, "Will you come and pray for him?"

I averred, "I will come, but he has wronged the whole church, and I am not coming alone. I am not coming unless I can bring the whole church with me."

She cried, "Let me go ask him." She returned to the phone, shouting, "Bring them all!"

Now, let me digress to explain what had made him so angry. At a Sunday morning service, he told me that he owed God $400 back tithes and asked me what he should do. I told him that he should pay it. I continued, "If you don't pay it, God will not get the money, but you will not be able to keep it either. Somehow you will lose it." That very Sunday afternoon, lightning struck his two best horses, for which he had recently paid exactly $400, and killed them. He publicly blamed me for getting his horses killed.

When his wife told me to bring the whole church with me, I could not get them all, but I rounded up about four hundred people. We filled every nook and cranny of that large farmhouse. The front and back porches were filled, and the yard was loaded with people, crowding toward the house as best they could. It looked like a scene for the beginning of a great revival.

The wife asked, "Brother Ward, come and pray for my husband. He is upstairs in bed."

I answered, "No, I have a chair fixed in the living room. Tell him to come down and sit in this chair. God is going to heal him."

She replied, "You don't understand; he is dying; he can't get out of bed."

"God will give him strength to get out of bed," I cried. I was very young then, nineteen years old, you understand, and very hard-boiled, I guess, for a youngster. I would not be so cruel now.

At any rate, pretty soon I saw the deacon coming down the stairs in his bathrobe and slippers, and a little skullcap that farmers wore to bed in those days. He sat in the living room. He declared, "Before Brother Ward prays for me, I want to make a confession. I want to ask him and the whole church to forgive me."

I asked his wife if she had any oil. She replied that she only had a quart bottle of olive oil. I said, "Bring it on."

After he asked the whole church to forgive him, I got so happy I forgot what I was doing. I took off his skullcap. He was completely bald. Not fully realizing what I was doing, I turned that quart bottle of olive oil upside down over his head and began to rub the oil into his bald head.

The oil flowed down over his shoulders and all over him. He came out of that chair shouting, jumping to his feet. He gave a kick, and one of his slippers hit the ceiling. He gave another kick, and another slipper hit the ceiling. He began to dance in the spirit. He danced in and out of one room after another. He kept shouting, "I am healed! I am healed!"

He came back to church the next service and was the very best deacon that I ever had anywhere. A couple of months later, he told me, "Brother Ward, there is something that I have meant to tell you. Do you know that when you prayed for me and anointed me with oil, it seemed to me that I could feel that oil flowing all over me."

I answered, "Brother, if there is anything that I am absolutely certain about, it is that you were well-oiled."

- 40 -

A Miracle Happened As I Was Going out the Door

I rented the old First Baptist Church building in Albuquerque, New Mexico, after they had built a new building. I had fifteen hundred people attending my revival. One night I told the Lord, "I must have three hundred dollars tonight, as I must pay an important bill in the morning," and I felt a real charge of faith that I would have the $300 when I left the church that night. However, the offering that night was only $290. Ten dollars was lacking.

I was sure that some person would come up and slip $10 into my hands, but person after person left the building. Finally the last person in the church left, and I was alone. I did not want to question God, but as I started to go out of the auditorium, I was thinking, "I felt sure that I would have the three hundred dollars that I need tonight." I was out in the foyer of the building by this time, and I saw what looked like a suit from the cleaners, hanging where people hung their coats.

I said, "Someone has forgotten a suit." I picked up the garment, and I saw that it was my suit, which a man who owned a cleaning establishment had picked up two or three nights earlier. I read the note which he had pinned to the plastic covering the suit, "There is no charge for cleaning; we were glad to clean this suit for you." I began to thank God for the cleaning job, and I found my fingers going into a side pocket of the suit. To my amazement, there was a ten dollar bill in the pocket and a note which read, "God told me to give you this ten dollars." I tell you, I had a "hallelujah breakdown" right there in the foyer. I knew that God had not forgotten my prayer, but He had tested me until the very last minute, when I was only a couple of feet from the outside door.

God has always seemed to work for me at the last minute. I asked Him, "Why, the last minute?" He seemed to tell me that it was the only way that He would get the glory for working the miracle. For if the miracle came easily, I would think that my intelligence, or my influence, or some power of my own had birthed the miracle. But when the miracle takes place at the last minute, then I absolutely know that the miracle has to come from God. For all my finances are exhausted; all my strength is dissipated. I am a "goner" without Christ.

Then I asked God, "Why is it all right for You to seek Your glory, and it is wrong for me to seek my glory?" And it seemed to me that God let me know that my glory represents impermanence, sinfulness, and an inability to bring things to pass, whereas His glory is eternal, anchored in holiness, speaks of perfection, and reveals a power to bring things to pass in total victory.

- 41 -

God Paid for a Six-Hundred-Mile Trip

In 1937, when I was twenty-one years old. I had just finished a three weeks revival for my brother-in-law and sister in Richmond, Virginia, and God told me to go to Taunton, Massachusetts, to hold a revival for Rev. A.A. August. I thought, Brother August has not written me and asked me to come, and I have never gone anywhere to conduct a revival without an invitation. But God spoke to me, "You are scheduled to start a revival there Tuesday night."

So I told my sister and brother-in-law, "I am packing my car and leaving for Taunton, Massachusetts." When I was ready to leave, my sister said, "Wait a few more minutes, because the mailman will soon be here, and maybe there will be a letter with some money in it for you." I had learned early to listen to my sister, so I waited. In a few minutes the mail arrived and, sure enough, there was a letter for me. I thought "God is sending me enough money to go to Massachusetts." But when I opened the letter, there was only two dollars in it. I knew that two dollars would not buy the gas for me to travel six hundred miles to Taunton, but God had told me to go, so I said, "I will buy two dollars worth of gas and trust God." I said good-bye to my folks and left.

I was driving between Richmond and Washington, D.C., and I saw a house by the side of the road. I remembered that in that house was a preacher friend of mine. I decided, "I am going to stop and say 'Hello.' " I knocked on the door, and when the preacher opened the door, I saw about four or five suitcases, all packed, sitting on the floor. I asked my friend, "Are you going somewhere?"

He replied, "Yes, my two coworkers and I have our suitcases all packed, and we are going to Providence, Rhode Island, to the Zion Bible College convention. God told us to get packed, that someone was coming by to drive us to Providence."

I answered, "Well, I am the 'someone,' for I am going to Providence and, fifteen miles on the other side of Providence, to Taunton, Massachusetts. You come, and I will be glad to take you."

The preacher said, "God told us to pay all of the gas and oil, and any other expenses."

I shouted, "Glory to God! Come on."

When we pulled on the Bible College grounds, Brother Augut came around a car, and seeing me, cried, "Thank God, you are here! For two weeks we have been announcing you to begin a revival at our church tomorrow night, Tuesday night. We did not know where you were in the world. We did not know how to contact you, but God told us to announce you to start Tuesday, and He would send you. So we have advertised you in the newspapers, and we have had posters printed, also, so you are all advertised."

I declared, "Yes, I am going to start the revival tomorrow night, but first I would like to go into the Bible College and attend the convention."

He said, "I want to give you a dollar and a quarter to buy some gas to get over to Taunton." (In those days, you could get eight gallons of gas for a dollar.)

I went into Zion Bible College, and Sister Christine A. Gibson, the President of Zion, which I had attended for three years, was receiving an offering. She said, "I am placing a Bible on the platform, and I want each of you to put your very best offering on the Bible."

I had a dollar and a quarter. So I went forward and put the quarter on the Bible, but God spoke to me, "You did not give Me your best offering. You had a dollar and a quarter. You kept the dollar and gave Me the quarter."

I replied, "Forgive me, Lord." I marched back to the front and placed the dollar on the Bible, too.

When I returned to my seat, a man put a piece of paper in my hand. I said, "God bless you." When I went to my car, I saw that the piece of paper was a check for $125. I had given God a dollar and a quarter, and He had given me $125. So once again, I saw that you can never outgive God. The more that you do for God, the more He does for you.

- 42 -

The Potato Story

I was holding a revival for my brother-in-law and sister in Quantico, Virginia, the home of the great United States Marine base, when I was seventeen years old. They were going through a severe financial struggle, and all that we had to eat was potatoes. I don't mean potatoes with meat, gravy and peas; I just mean potatoes. We had potatoes for breakfast, lunch and dinner; and if we had wanted a midnight snack, it would have still been potatoes. We had potatoes boiled, fried, baked, scrambled, but they were still potatoes. I had so many potatoes that I never wanted to look another one in the eye.

In my room, before dinner, after two weeks of eating potatoes, I bombarded Heaven with prayer, "Now, Lord, I command in the Name of Jesus, that there will be a good dinner on the table today. I am hungry." I felt that I had prayed through. So when my brother-in-law called me for dinner, I burst out of my room like a full-blown cyclone, alive with anticipation. But, then, I stopped short, because there was only one bowl on the table, and that was heaped and running over with boiled potatoes.

I sat at my usual place at the table, and my brother-in-law said, "Bill, ask God to bless the food."

I said to myself, "Food, there isn't any food. All we have is potatoes. How can I be a hypocrite and bless these potatoes, when I don't want to be near them?"

My brother-in-law noticed my reticence to pray. He repeated, "Preacher, ask God to bless the food."

I was saying in my heart, "I can't be a hypocrite and bless these potatoes," when God spoke to me as distinctly and clearly as I have ever heard Him. He declared, "In everything give thanks; for this is the will of God in Christ Jesus, concerning you."

Well, I began to bless those potatoes, and I blessed them upside down and around about sideways. I thanked God for the farmers in Aroostook County, Maine, who planted the potatoes. I thanked God for the men who picked the potatoes, put them in barrels, and set the barrels on trucks. I thanked God for the truck drivers who drove the potatoes into town, and I thanked God for the merchants who sold the potatoes in the stores. I thanked God for the people who bought and brought them to the preachers' house. I thanked God for the preachers who cooked the potatoes and put them on the table. I was only halfway through my prayer, when there was a knock at the door. You wouldn't believe how fast I said, "Amen."

My brother-in-law, my sister, and I ran to the door. To this day I don't know which one of us opened the door. There was a man standing there, and he cried, "Here is a basket of food. I have a second basket of food at the bottom of the stairs, and I have a third basket in the car." He brought the three baskets of food into the house. There were all kinds of food in the baskets, everything but you know what. Then my brother-in-law went over and took the potatoes off the table and said, "Wife, fix the dinner."

My sister fixed the meal, and we had a wonderful, wonderful dinner that day. Now my brother-in-law and sister had learned their lesson before. They had gone three weeks with nothing to eat but peanuts, and had learned that in whatsoever state they found themselves to be content and thankful for all things. But as a teenager, this was my first experience, and God had to teach me that in everything I should give thanks.

- 43 -

My Sister Put the Children on the Porch

My sister and brother-in-law had been without food on several occasions. One time my sister had to put the children on the back porch, because she felt that they might ask for food when the company came. They had been without food all day.

One time my sister said, "All right, children, it's time to go to bed."

They answered, "Mama, we haven't even had our breakfast yet."

You see some of us have paid a great price for our ministry. We have not been in this work of God for the money; for there was not any money in it. The miracle is that, today, my sister and her family feed thousands of people free in America, Israel and in other places.

They have a large campmeeting in Ashland, Virginia, fifteen miles north of Richmond, where people come from all over the world. Many times, I have counted people from forty-five or more different nations there on a given night, and there is no charge for food and lodging at the camp.

All the preachers that I know, with the exception of a very few, have known tremendous hardships. We are out to work for Jesus, no matter what the cost. I heard the late Brother Guy Shields, an old time Texas evangelist, say that he had preached the first year and a half for a dollar and a half. I told him that I had preached the first three and a half years for nothing and a half.

I have always remembered the first offering that I ever received. I had preached a revival in Painter, Maryland, speaking every night for five weeks. In the last service, a deacon stood and said, "I am placing a Bible on the altar. If anyone wants to give Brother Ward an offering for these five weeks of preaching, just place it on the Bible. I received $5.50. I was so happy that I wrote home about it.

- 44 -

The Bill Was Paid Out of a Rat's Nest

One day, my brother-in-law, Wallace H. Heflin, Sr. needed $12 in order to pay a bill. We all began to pray that he would get this money immediately. God told him to pull a loose board off the bottom of the old church wall. He did and found a rat's nest. A rat had been taking dollar bills out of the church offerings and had made a nest out of the money. Brother Heflin began to scrape the nest and the floor around the nest. He gathered the bits and pieces of money and took them to the United States Treasury Building in Washington, D.C., twenty-seven miles away. They gave him $12 for it, the exact amount that we were praying for, in order to pay his bill.

- 45 -

A Nosebleed That Helped Get a Boy Saved

When I was nineteen, I went to Winchester, Virginia, to attend a tent meeting being conducted by a great friend of mine, Richard Bishop. He and I, as boys, were in the same Sunday school class in Washington, D.C. When he saw me enter the tent, Brother Bishop said, "I am glad to have Brother Ward here tonight, and we want him to preach for us."

I walked to the platform, stood behind the pulpit, and opened my Bible, but God told me that I was not to preach. So I closed my Bible, saying, "Brother Bishop, God just told me that I am not to preach tonight."

When I arrived back at my seat, my nose began to bleed. I took my handkerchief and tried to stem the flow of blood, but was unsuccessful, so I walked out of the tent. As soon as I was outside, my nose stopped bleeding. Several times I started back into the tent, but each time my nose would start bleeding again. God told me that He had caused me to come out of the tent for a purpose and to stand still, and I would discover what the purpose was.

I stood outside the tent for forty-five minutes while Brother Bishop preached. It looked terrible, because I was a visiting preacher, who had driven eighty-five miles to hear Richard Bishop preach. There was a rather small crowd that night, and I, a visiting preacher, was standing outside the tent.

As Brother Bishop finished his message, and was giving the altar call, I saw a young man climb over a fence that bordered the highway, walk about a hundred yards across the field and stand next to me. He stood there as Brother Bishop continued with his altar call. Then God spoke distinctly to me, saying, "I made your nose bleed. I brought you out of the tent; I had you stand here for forty-five minutes; and, for forty-five minutes, I have been bringing this man across town to you; and you have not asked him to go to the altar."

I turned quickly to the young man and asked, "Would you like to go to the altar, kneel down and pray, and give your heart to Jesus?"

He replied, "I certainly would."

I went with the fellow to the altar. God told me how to pray, that he was a prodigal son and had been away on a far journey, but his Christian mother was praying for him, and now he was coming home.

After the young man was converted, he told me, "I was going into a liquor store all the way across town, and I felt a hand on my shoulder, and a voice told me not to go into that liquor store. Then that hand on my shoulder led me across town, caused me to climb the fence, and come and stand next to you."

Then I told the fellow, "I will pay for the long distance call. I want you to phone your mother and tell her that you have come to Jesus."

He called his mother more than a thousand miles way, and I heard him say, "Mom, I have come home; I have been converted and have come back to Jesus."

- 46 -

They Came To Kill One Another, but God ...

I conducted a revival in Pokomoke City, Maryland, in 1938, when I was twenty-two years old. The first Sunday morning that I was there, I began preaching on the need for unity in order to have a revival. Unbeknownst to me, there was a man, sitting on a back seat, who had a revolver, and had come to kill a man sitting on a front seat. The man in the front had a package of lye, which he intended to throw in the other fellow's face. They hated each other though they came to the same church.

In the middle of my sermon, I began saying things that the two men knew I could not have known in the natural, as it was my first service there. While I was preaching, I saw the man in the back come running down the main aisle, and at the same time the fellow in the front started running toward the back, down the same aisle. They met in the middle of the church, fell on their knees, crying, hugging each other, and asking one another for forgiveness.

When the people of the church saw that, the entire congregation arose as one body and ran to the front of the church. As many as could fell at the altar; the rest of the people knelt between the seats all over the church, praying and crying to God.

After church, the pastor said, “Now I know that we are going to have a real revival, for these two men have been full of hate for each other for a long time.” I stayed there three weeks, preaching every night, and we had a wonderful revival.

- 47 -

Love Conquers All

Then I went to preach in another church in Kitzmiller, Maryland, where I also preached nightly for three weeks. Toward the end of the crusade, a little girl came to me, saying, “My mother is dying up in that little white cottage on the hill. Would you come and pray for her?”

I went up and knocked on the door. A huge, burly man came to the door and asked, “Aren’t you from that church down in the valley?”

I answered, "That is right."

He cried, "Well, nobody from that church is going to pray for my wife."

I asked, "Why?"

He continued, "The deacon of that church, who leads song service every night, he and I have hated each other for twenty years. He has tried to ruin me, and I have tried to ruin him. No, sir, nobody from that church is going to pray for my wife."

I asked the big fellow, "If I go get that deacon, and he asks you to forgive him, will you forgive him?"

He bellowed, "No!"

I put my foot in the door as he tried to close it and began praying at the top of my voice, "Oh, God, have mercy on this man. He is a terrible hypocrite. He would rather see his wife die than to get right with another Christian."

The giant of a man grabbed me and said, "Be quiet, man, all my neighbors are listening to you. The windows are going up, the doors are opening, and people are coming out on the street. They are all listening to you, and you are going to ruin my reputation."

I began to pray all the louder. You have to remember that I was only twenty-two years old. I may have a little more mercy today. As I prayed, he quickly cried, "You go get that deacon, and we will make it right somehow."

I found the deacon painting some buildings in his back yard. I affirmed, "Deacon, I am thoroughly ashamed of you. I have conducted a three-week revival here. You have led the singing every night, and you hate this man up on the hill. I want you to go with me and make it right. Ask him to forgive you."

He retorted, "I will not do it."

Now, he was a little fellow, and I was not a bit afraid of him. I held his shoulders, and glued him to the ground, and began to pray at the top of my voice. I said, "Oh, God, have mercy on this hypocrite. He has led the song service every night in my revival, and he hates a man in this town."

He whispered, "Brother Ward, please keep quiet. My neighbors are listening to you. I hear windows and doors opening. Please, you will ruin my reputation."

I prayed all the louder.

He said, "Please keep quiet, and I will go with you."

So he and I went up to see the big fellow on the hill. When we knocked on his door, the minute that door opened, the little man cried, "Please forgive me."

The big man said, "Forgive me, too, and come in."

The two men and I got on our knees on the parlor floor. They cried together and hugged each other. Their tears mingled in a common pool on the floor.

I went over to the dying woman on the bed and said, "In the name of Jesus, you can get up now. God only let you get sick to bring these two men together. Now they are together, and you are healed." She arose, perfectly healed, and cooked us a wonderful dinner, and we all sat down and ate together in fellowship.

- 48 -

A Champion Is Made

I was invited to dinner at the home of friends in Saginaw, Michigan. As we were talking in the living room, the mother told her little son, three or four years old, to run over and turn the TV off; and in a moment she asked him to run back and turn the TV on. Then she turned to me, saying, "You don't know why I told my son to do that, do you?"

I answered, "No, I really do not."

She said, "When my boy was just a year or so old, his feet were club feet. His feet turned in until you held him and prayed for him. You asked God to heal his feet and let him grow up to become a champion baseball and football player, and make him the best ball player in the high schools of Saginaw. I just wanted you to see how he can run since God healed his feet."

About twelve or thirteen years later, I was holding another revival in Saginaw and was invited to the same home for dinner. The mother brought out a large newspaper article with the boy's picture in it. The paper stated that he had been voted the best baseball and football player in the high schools of Saginaw, Michigan. She said, "Your prayer was surely answered."

- 49 -

An Unexpected Ten Dollars

One Sunday, my wife and I left home in Tulsa, to start a revival in Shawnee, Oklahoma. As we were starting our car, the next door neighbor ran out, crying, "Wait a minute," and he handed me $10.

I was surprised, as he had never given us anything before. I said to my wife, "This is the first time that God ever sent me money, when I did not need it." But God knew what we needed better than we did, because we had to travel on the Oklahoma Turnpike. When we stopped to pay the toll, I found that the only money that we had was the $10 the neighbor had given me. Then later, we had to buy gas, and the rest of the $10 was spent. We arrived at the church in Shawnee, realizing that if God had not spoken to our neighbor, we would not have arrived in time to begin our revival that night.

- 50 -

He Acted Just Like An Angel, Anyway

I left home in Tulsa, Oklahoma, to begin a revival. As I got out on the turnpike, I had a flat tire. I sat there, and thought, "Dear God, I am the dumbest boy You have, but I am still Your boy. I have a spare tire in the trunk, but I don't have any tools with which to change the tire."

Just then, a man drove up and parked his car behind me. He said, "Give me the key to your trunk."

I answered, "Well, I have a spare tire in the trunk, but I don't have any tools."

He said, "I've got tools, so I'll change it and save you the trouble."

I handed him the key to my trunk, and I never saw anybody change a tire so fast in my life. Seems like all he did was speak a word or two to me while he was changing it and the tire was completely changed. He handed my key back and I said "How much do I owe you, sir?"

He replied, "Just thank the Father." He got in his car, started down the highway, and I saw him turn around and go back the opposite way.

I am not saying that was an angel, but he acted just like an angel, and I needed help because I was in distress. I had to preach that night, and I don't know how I could have reached the church in time to preach if he had not come along. But he did come along, and it blessed me.

And I did thank the Father. I thanked Him for always being so wonderful to us.

Isn't it glorious to know that God has Christians and angels who can work for Him and do His bidding? He sends them to be a blessing to us, and I imagine every one of you have been blessed by an angel many times when you didn't even know it.

- 51 -

The Wife of the Chief Justice of the Supreme Court

The deacons waited on me before church, saying, "Now when you preach tonight, please be on your very best behavior because we have the wife of the Chief Justice of the Supreme Court in the service tonight."

I tried to be dignified, but in the middle of my sermon, the Spirit of God came on me, and I jumped down off the platform, went back and put my hand on the head of the wife of the Chief Justice of the Supreme Court and prayed for her. She arose to her feet, shouting and praising God. Then she was baptized in the Holy Ghost, speaking in a beautiful, heavenly language.

When she could finally speak English, she said, "This is what I have been looking for all of my life, for fifty years. I just returned from India, where I was looking for a religion that would satisfy me. I never found that which my soul yearned for until tonight. This is what I want. I like an old-fashioned Holy Ghost meeting like this. Glory to God!"

- 52 -

"You Have Disgraced the Clergy Today"

I preached at a campmeeting in West Virginia, and when I finished shouting and praising God, a man waited on me at the platform, saying, "I am an Advent Preacher; and before I leave the campground, I want to tell you that you have disgraced the clergy today."

Quick as I could, I put my hand on his head and prayed, "Dear Lord, Give him a double portion of what you just gave me."

That man hit the floor and became a holy roller. He rolled back and forth and made a lot of noise. After praising God for more than an hour, he began to speak in a heavenly language.

When he came over to say good-bye to me, he started to hug me, but I pushed him back, saying, "Sir, I'm a Pentecostal preacher, and I'm about to leave the campground, but before I leave the campground, I want to tell you that you disgraced the clergy today."

He threw his arms around me and hugged me, crying, "Oh, brother, I never knew how wonderful it is."

I replied, "That's just it. Those who want a quiet, dignified religion just don't know what it's like when the Holy Ghost gets hold of your soul and turns you inside out for God. Hallelujah! You feel that if you don't shout, you will explode. Glory be to God!"

- 53 -

A Cool Breeze Blows in the Desert

One day, at home in Richmond, Virginia, my nose was bleeding, and we could not get the blood stopped. The blood continued to flow for some time. I was lying on the bathroom tile floor in shock, shaking all over. So my wife called the rescue squad and had me taken to the hospital.

The doctor declared, "It's a good thing they brought you to the hospital; you have lost half the blood in your body." He cauterized my nose, burned it so it would quit bleeding, and then he filled my nose full of cotton.

I said, "Hurry up, doctor, I have to be on the airplane in two hours to go to Bakersfield, California, and hold a revival meeting."

The doctor laughed and averred, "You will not be on any airplane in two hours. You will be in bed."

But I was on the airplane in two hours and went to Bakersfield to conduct a revival for Rev. Danny Davis.

When I arrived at Bakersfield with my nose still filled with cotton, Brother Davis said, "Oh, Brother Ward, I am sorry that I asked you to come to Bakersfield at this time. Because it is so hot, the people will not come out to hear you preach in the tent. It has been 115 to 120 degrees every night, and the people cannot stand it under a tent. You know that Bakersfield is in the Mojave Desert, and it gets hot and stays hot here." I replied, "Brother Davis, it is not going to be hot while I am here. I have already talked to God about the heat." That night, at the beginning of the service, a wonderful cool breeze blew through the tent and, from then on, the entire time that I was there, we had nice cool weather and a great revival.

After the revival meeting, Brother Davis declared, "Brother Ward, of all the revivals that you have held for me, this was the greatest."

- 54 -

I Am Able to Preach

I never had a nosebleed from that time on until my next birthday. At that time, I was conducting a revival meeting in Gettysburg, Pennsylvania, and my nose started bleeding just before church. I called the preacher to come pray for me, and he said, "Your blood is like water; it's just pouring out of your nose."

I said, "You pray for me."

God stopped my nose bleed, but the next night my nose started bleeding again, just before church. I cried, "Dear God, you called me to preach, and the devil is trying to keep me from preaching; I'm going to church, and if you want me to preach, my nose will stop bleeding so I can preach." I went to church, and my nose stopped bleeding. Glory be to God!

- 55 -

Just About Everyone Was Telling Me How to Die

When I had blood clots in my right leg, seemingly everyone was telling me how to die. Some people came to our house. You know the cousins, grandchildren and great grandchildren of Job's friends are still around. They seemed to congregate at our house. They told me stories like, "I hate to tell you this, but the man next door had what you have, and he died." "Our mailman had blood clots in his legs, and the blood clots went to his lungs, and he is confined to a wheelchair." They went down the line, and I listened to the wrong voices.

Sometimes I want to bend over and tell someone to kick me for listening to the wrong voices. I stayed in bed for six weeks because I listened to people who said, "You cannot stand on that leg; it may kill you." They told me, "You have to stay in bed with your leg propped up on three pillows, so that it is elevated." I found out later that was the worse thing I could have done, but I was listening to them. I thought they knew what they were talking about.

After spending six weeks in bed, one day I was reaching for the telephone which my wife had left on my bed. I was going to call Rev. Bill Bishop in Saginaw, Michigan, and tell him, "I am sorry; I can't come to hold a revival for you, because I am confined to bed." But God spoke to me, saying, "Get out of bed, pack your suitcases, go to Saginaw, Michigan, and hold that revival."

After listening to all those doubting Thomas' voices for six weeks, when I heard the voice of God, I knew what it was. I knew it was authoritative. It was just like when God spoke the worlds into existence. There was power and authority in His voice.

I jumped out of bed, packed my suitcases, and left that same day for Michigan. After the revival services, Brother Bishop told me, "You have held me five or six revivals, but this was the greatest revival that you ever held for me."

I answered, "It was the greatest revival, because God shook me, motivated me and thrust me out of bed."

I have never gone back to that bed for more than eight hours at a time since. Praise the Lord! If I had continued to listen to the wrong voices, I would probably still be in bed.

You have your choice of which way you are going to go. I am placing my address with the people who believe that God can do anything. Although He can work any miracle, if you are to get something from God, you still have to take it. The challenge is to go into action. Do something. Stop talking about how much faith you have and act now.

- 56 -

Let Me Spend My Last Night on Earth in Church

In 1937, I was conducting a revival meeting in Durham, North Carolina. During a night service, we felt a wind blow over the church. As the wind would blow from one direction, the entire congregation began to sway this way, and the wind would blow back, and the congregation would sway that way.

In the middle of this wonderful presence of God, they brought a woman into church that the doctors said would die before the night was over. They carried her in, put a pillow on a front pew, and sat her on a pillow. I saw Jesus walk right in front of that woman, and I said "Sister, Jesus is walking in front of you right now, reach out your hand and touch Him."

I saw a little bony, gaunt hand go out, and I saw her touch Jesus, and when she touched Him, she came out of that seat. Glory be to God! She began waving that pillow. She was jumping and praising God.

Then she told us her story. She had been in a TB sanitarium for years, and that morning, four doctors had said, "You will never live through the night. So go home and spend the last night that you have on earth with your family."

The relatives were called. They got the old model Ford and took her home. About twenty-five people, most of them members of her family, gathered at home to spend the last night with Grandma, but Grandma said, "If this is my last night on earth, I want to spend it in church." So all the folks brought Grandma to the church where I was conducting the revival services.

You know, that Grandma was healed. I received a letter from her ten years later. She affirmed, "I am still living, and I just hung a big washing on the line in the backyard, and I thought I would come in the house, write you a letter and tell you that I am still alive and still healed. Hallelujah!"

Yes, my God is able to turn things around.

- 57 -

Cross-Eyes Straightened

A man came to me in Providence, Rhode Island. His name was Barton Whitall. He cried, "I am cross-eyed. I have been cross-eyed all my life, and I want you to pray that God will straighten my eyes."

We were on the third floor, and the Spirit of God came on him as I prayed. With his eyes closed, he put his foot out to go down the steps. I think the angels must have carried him. I don't know if he touched a step, but when he reached the second floor landing, his eyes were perfectly straight. Hallelujah!

- 58 -

The Night That I Was Hit with a Slight Stroke

One night, when I was 77 years old, I was hit with a slight stroke. I prayed, "Lord, I would rather die than live the rest of my life with the results of a stroke." My left arm seemed as heavy as lead; I could not lift it. My left leg was so heavy that I could not use it. When I tried to stand, I would fall down.

My wife said to me, "You cannot die tonight."

I asked the Lord to let me go to sleep, have a good night's sleep, and awake in the morning completely healed. That is exactly what happened. I awoke the next morning completely healed with no aftereffects of a stroke. That day, I went to the YMCA and played handball as though nothing had happened.

- 59 -

The Woman a Hundred Thousand People Called 'Mother'

Lillian Trasher was going to get married. She went to New York City to meet her fiancé, but the Lord told her to go to Egypt as a missionary. She took the engagement ring off, handed it to her fiancé and said, "I am sorry, I love you, but I can't marry you. God has called me to be a candle in Egypt, and I must go to that country and burn out for Jesus."

We rode the train along the Nile River all day, when we went to Lillian Trasher's orphanage in Assiout, Egypt. We arrived at the orphanage at 11 o'clock at night, and we thought, nobody will even come to the door and let us in at this hour. And we don't know where we can find a place to spend the night. But, suddenly all the lights flashed on everywhere, and eleven hundred children came out of the orphanage at eleven o'clock at night and started singing:

"Jesus loves the little children,
All the children of the world.
Red and yellow, black and white,
They are precious in His sight."

Who taught them that song? A woman who had never been married, and yet had chosen to be their mother. When Lillian Trasher died, the Egyptian newspaper headlines stated, "Lillian Trasher, the woman that 100,000 Egyptians call 'Mother,' has passed on to her reward."

- 60-

There Is A Whole Case of the Milk in the Attic

I held a revival meeting in Charlotte, North Carolina, at the Garr Auditorium. I was so captivated by the story of Dr. A.G. Garr, that I wrote his life story.

A.G. Garr is credited with being the first Pentecostal missionary to China. He went to Kowloon, and that is why when I could not get a hotel room in Hong Kong, I went over gladly across the water to Kowloon and got a hotel room there, because I remembered how Dr. Garr had met God in Kowloon.

A.G. Garr had a little baby boy who became, in his adult life, one of my best friends. His name was Alfred, and he used to sing on the Texaco Fire Chief coast-to-coast radio program many years ago. Then he was converted and became a wonderful preacher, finally pastoring the church in Charlotte, North Carolina, which his father started.

But I want to tell you of an instance which took place in Kowloon, when Alfred was a little baby. He was dying. A.G. Garr looked up to God, praying, "God, you did not bring me from America to China to see my little boy die because we cannot get the milk for his formula." Everywhere that Dr. Garr went, the grocer would say, "There is no Borden's Eagle brand milk in the whole country of China, and there is certainly none in Kowloon."

A.G. Garr looked up to God, and God said, "You go to a certain street, and you will find a grocery store on that corner. You go into that grocery store, and they will have a whole case of Borden's Eagle brand milk in the attic."

So Dr. Garr went over to the grocery store and said to the grocer, "I have come to get some Borden's Eagle brand canned milk."

The owner of the store replied, "We don't have a

can, there is not a can of that Eagle brand milk in all of Kowloon."

A.G. Garr answered, "Listen, God told me that you have a whole case of it in the attic."

The man replied, "You go up there, and if you find anything there you can keep all of it. You won't have to pay for it."

Dr. Garr went in the attic and found a whole case of Borden's Eagle brand milk that had never been opened. He brought it down, and the grocer said, "You don't have to pay me for it. It made me feel good just to know that God knows where my store is, and what I have in it."

Hallelujah! God will supply your needs if you let your light shine. If you let people know you are a Christian, God is going to pay your debts, shoulder your burdens, solve your problems, and meet your needs. Yes, He is going to work some miracles for you, too.

- 61 -

Miracles Under Wigglesworth

I saw miracles under Wigglesworth. Brother Wigglesworth was a very stern man. One day they brought a woman from the hospital, dying of cancer. She was almost skin and bones; she had cancer of the stomach. Her doctor came from the hospital to see that they took proper care of her.

The ushers brought her to Brother Wigglesworth, who in the process of praying for her, and overcome with a hatred for the devil who had given her cancer, hit her in the stomach. The noise was so loud that it seemed that you could hear it all over the auditorium, where seven thousand people were assembled.

The doctor jumped up and started screaming "We are going to sue you! We are going to sue you! You have killed my patient! Look at her; she is dead!"

Brother Wigglesworth said, "She is not dead. She is healed. Sit down and be quiet."

In a few minutes that woman got out of the bed and began to walk all over the platform, shouting, "I am healed! I am healed!"

I'll tell you, our God is a worker of miracles.

- 62 -

A Wigglesworth Meeting

I remember one time when my parents took me to a Wigglesworth revival, when I was five or six years old; but actually, you know, your personality never considers your age. I think of these things happening to me when I was five or six years old as things that happened to me just yesterday, for my personality is the same, and I am going to live for all eternity. I might look at some of you people and think, "My, they are getting old," but I don't think I am getting old. Amen!

I remember when this woman came into the revival service; she couldn't walk. Brother Wigglesworth said, "Run!"

She answered, "It is all I can do to stand up, and I have to hold onto something in order to stand."

Brother Wigglesworth shouted, "Don't talk back to me, woman! I said to run. You do what I say!"

That woman took off running. She ran all around that auditorium, skipping, jumping and shouting, "I'm healed! I'm healed!"

Now, as for you, you might as well reach out for your miracle now. It is out there, but you have to make an effort. Don't sit down and wait for the miracle to come to you. You start looking for the miracle and expecting it to come. And do whatever you can do to help make it come. If you could not raise your arm, start raising it. If you could not walk, start walking. Praise the Lord!

- 63 -

He Meant to Slit My Throat from Ear to Ear

I was holding a revival for Danny Davis in Bakersfield, California. He had rented the auditorium in the Bakersfield Inn. They had given me a room in the Inn, back in a section all by itself. It was a section where Hollywood had made quite a few moving picture shows, because that part of the motel looked like a place for cowboy pictures. I was the only one renting a room in the whole wing.

A man had said, "I am going to catch that preacher when he goes to church tonight." I had to walk from my wing across the yard to the auditorium where I was preaching. The man had said, "I am going to hide behind the bushes, and when that preacher comes out, I am going to slit his throat."

Well, unbeknownst to me, a doctor had come into the motel. Since they did not have a place to put him, they put him in the wing where I was. When the doctor came out in the dark, headed for the auditorium, the man who was going to slit my throat, mistook the doctor for me. He jumped on him and slit his throat from ear to ear.

I had gone early, and this man came out when I normally would have come out. They came into the auditorium, crying, "Come quickly, there is a man out here with his throat slit from ear to ear."

When I got there, I put my hand on his head and prayed, "God, I command this blood to stop flowing, and I command him to be healed right now in the Name of Jesus." I went back into the auditorium.

They called an ambulance and took this man to the hospital. The men in the ambulance said, "He will die before he gets to the hospital."

But he did not die, and when he arrived at the hospital, they examined him and said, "We don't know what happened, but the blood has stopped; there is no bleeding. Why, we don't even have to sew his neck, for that has healed up, also."

When I came out of the auditorium after preaching, the doctor was standing there, waiting for me. He affirmed, "I want to thank you for praying for me. God healed me. Look, I don't even have a scar."

How can people live without God? I appreciate God. I have seen Him do so many wonderful miracles.

- 64 -

The Vision of Winning Children for God

It was Saturday afternoon in Washington, D.C., and I was preparing my sermon for Sunday. To my dismay, it seemed that all the children in the neighborhood had congregated in my front yard, and they were making so much noise that I went to the door and said, "You kids scram! Get going! I'm studying for a sermon. I have to preach in the morning."

It was just like God slapped me, and said, "Suffer the little children to come unto me and forbid them not, for of such is the kingdom of Heaven."

I quickly cried, "Wait a minute, children, I have just been converted. I am going to the store and buy some cake, ice cream, candy and pop, and I will be back to give all of you some."

They not only stayed; they multiplied. I had about twenty-five children when I left, and I had about fifty children when I returned. I sat them down in the front yard, and I told them the story of David killing Goliath. I gave them pop and cookies and candy.

When I finished with that story, they cried, "Tell us another one." I gave them some candy and cookies and I told them another story. They affirmed, "We like this." So I started having church in my front yard every Saturday. Glory be to God!

You have to remember that God loves the children. One lady heard me preach in Corpus Christi, Texas, about winning the children. She caught the vision from me, and when she returned to her home in Palestine, Texas, she began having children's meetings in her home. Thirty-five preachers are preaching the gospel today because of attending her children's services.

Time is a continuum, and time marches on. The children you have around you now will be the preachers of tomorrow. Judah declared, *"For how shall I go up to my father, and the lad be not with me?"* (Genesis 44:34). How can we go to Heaven, and the children be not with us?

- 65 -

Jack Coe Could Not Get into His Own Revival

I was with Jack Coe in Philadelphia, Pennsylvania. He was holding a revival in the Met. It seated five thousand people. Jack Coe and I arrived in a taxi cab. When we reached the side door, a fireman would not let us enter. He said, "This building seats five thousand people, and it is packed to the rafters. No one else can get in."

Jack Coe told the fireman, "I'm the evangelist; they can't have church without me. They are all sitting in there waiting for me."

The fireman replied, "I don't care who you are; you are not going in there. The fire regulations won't allow another person in there."

It took Jack Coe forty-five minutes to get in, where he was scheduled to preach, and I never got into the building that day myself.

- 66 -

The President of Phillips Petroleum

In 1942, I was holding a revival meeting in Bartlesville, Oklahoma. The city was the home of Frank Phillip. He and his brother were head of Phillips 66 Petroleum. They were multimillionaires.

Frank Phillips' valet was converted in my revival meeting. So every time he would help Frank Phillips with his clothes, and so forth, he would tell him what I preached the night before. Soon Frank Phillips wanted to see me. He was seventy-seven years old at the time and would not live too much longer.

The valet and I did everything we could, seeking to get Frank Phillips converted, but he kept saying, "I can't see it, I just can't see it. I wish I could see it, but I can't see it." He may have died without God, a multimillionaire, but perhaps without God. I think about it so much. In the natural, he had everything in this world, but he could not see what is so plain to me.

How wonderfully simple God made it for us to be converted! I am so glad that I have spiritual insight.

- 67 -

"It Is in the Top Drawer in the Dresser"

I was holding a revival in Austin, Texas, for Brother and Sister Harold and Eva Ansel. One day they invited me to their house for dinner. I had never been in their home before. Sister Ansel said to me, "If thou be a prophet of God tell me where the paper is that I can't find. I have been hunting for it for three days, and I must have it."

I was busy reading and didn't even look up. I answered, "It is in the top drawer in the dresser in the bathroom." I had never been in that bathroom, and I didn't know they had a dresser in there; but you see the Holy Ghost inside of me took up the challenge. For she had declared, "If thou be a prophet of God, tell me where that paper is."

Sister Ansel replied, "Ha, ha, I know you are not a prophet now, because I just looked in that drawer, and the paper isn't there." But she added, "I think I will look again."

Soon she came out screaming, "You must be a prophet of God! The paper was in that drawer!"

So men of God sometimes know things. People ask, "How did you know that?"

"I don't know how I knew it, but I knew it." In my opinion, our minds contact the mind of God; and since God knew where the paper was, He revealed it to me to meet the challenge of the moment.

- 68 -

"With That Kind of Faith You Will Walk Today"

In 1951, I conducted a city-wide revival in my large tent in Albuquerque, New Mexico. The tent, larger than a football field, was pitched on the fairgrounds. One evening, I saw four men carrying a bed to the tent. I walked over and saw that a woman was lying on the bed. I asked her what was wrong.

She answered, "I've been paralyzed for ten years. I have never been able to flex a finger or move a toe in all this time." She continued, "But, I am going to be healed tonight. I have told these four men, who are carrying me, that I will not need them after church, for I am going to walk home. And every night, the rest of the revival, I am going to walk to the tent and walk home."

I replied, "Sister, with that kind of faith, you are going to walk today." I prayed for her right there, outside the tent. God came upon that woman and healed her. She got off the bed and went leaping and shouting into church. Every evening I would see her walking to the services and then walking home afterwards.

Certainly, I must reiterate that I am no healer. I could not have healed this woman. God is the Healer. Only He can work such miracles. To God be the Glory. I believe further that God has a miracle for you. He is no respecter of persons. What He did for one, He will do for you, if you meet the same conditions.

- 69 -

The Steering Wheel Came Off in His Hands

In 1955, I was conducting a revival in Shawnee, Oklahoma. One night in church, the pastor told me that there was a telephone call for me. I answered it, and a doctor in the hospital informed me that a member of the church was driving home from work; and the steering wheel came off in his hands. The car left the road, hit a tree, and the man had his neck broken in three places. Three doctors said that he might not live through the night. But the man kept crying, "Get Evangelist Ward over here to pray for me."

I interrupted the doctor, stating, "I am on my way." I told the pastor, "Keep the service going until I get back."

At the hospital, I prayed for the fellow. Then I called the doctor in, saying, "Please x-ray this man again. I have prayed for him, and he wants to go back to the church service with me."

The doctor answered, "We just x-rayed the man."

I replied, "X-ray him again, please."

Pretty soon the doctor came back, saying, "We don't know what happened. Our x-ray machine must have been broken, for this man does not have a broken neck." The fellow got dressed and went to church with me.

- 70 -

Sobered Up, Saved and Healed of a Broken Back

I was conducting a revival crusade in Lufkin, Texas. One night they brought a man to the service who was drunk. He had a broken back, and he was in a body cast from his neck to his feet. They laid him on the altar. He looked at me, and said, "Preacher, I'm drunk, and I have a broken back. Can you get me saved?"

I answered, "You will be saved, and the same God who saves you, can heal you." After I prayed for him, I was busy praying for someone else. I did not know it, but he asked several deacons to carry him into a back room and cut the cast off his body. (If I had known what they were doing, I probably would not have allowed them to cut the cast off, because it was at a time when medical doctors were accusing preachers of practicing medicine without a license.)

But there he came back into the main auditorium, carrying this long cast. He was sober and converted. God filled him with the Holy Spirit and called him to preach. He built a new church in Diebald, Texas, and I had the privilege of dedicating the new church to God.

- 71 -

"We Are Going to Chase You Out of Town"

I was holding a revival in Alexandria, Virginia. We had seven hundred people a night for seven weeks. I said, "I have to close the revival this Sunday because I have to start a revival in Oskaloosa, Iowa, on Tuesday night."

Everybody begged me not to go. They said, "How can you leave a revival like this? We have seven hundred people coming every night, how can you leave it and go to Iowa?"

When I got out to Iowa, there were only thirty-five people there, and I thought, I guess I should have listened to some of those people. But God told me, "You are going to have a greater revival here than you had in Alexandria, Virginia."

God began to work, and one Sunday night two men waited on me at the platform, just before the service started. One man said, "I am the mayor of the city, and this man with me is Chief Councilman Smith, and we are ordering you to get out of town."

I replied, "What have I done?"

The mayor said, "You tell him, Councilman."

Councilman Smith averred, "I had the best factory in this city until you came. I have three hundred people working for me, and all three hundred have been saved in your meetings, except the janitor. Now when I go into my factory they are praising God; they make me feel like a sinner in my own factory. We are not going to put up with it. We are going to chase you out of town."

I kept right on preaching every night that week, and the next Sunday they came back.

The mayor declared, "We ordered you out of town."

I retorted, "God ordered me to stay in town. Who am I supposed to listen to, the mayor or the King?"

He said, "Well, you be in my office tomorrow at three o'clock."

I affirmed, "I will be there, and I will bring the pastor of this church with me."

So the pastor, Max Johnson, and I went to the mayor's office at three o'clock. The mayor had a telephone call and had to leave the room. I was walking around the room, and I saw a telegram on his desk. He had sent a telegram to the chief of police of my home town, Washington, D.C., and said, "Tell me something bad about William A. Ward, because I am going to run him out of town."

I saw the telegram that the chief of police sent back, asking, "Who is William A. Ward? Is he a white man or a black man?" I tell you I began to shout. I was happy that I was traveling incognito, they didn't know anything about me, good or bad. I could have told them some bad things about myself, but they didn't ask me.

When the mayor came in and sat down, Councilman Smith sat down, also, and the Spirit of God came upon me. I began to walk around the room, speaking in other tongues. When I walked by the councilman, he said, "Preacher, I told you everyone in my factory got saved except the janitor, and you told me you were going home and pray all night that the janitor would get saved. He got saved the next day."

That just added fuel to the fire, and I began to praise God even more. He continued, "Preacher, everybody has been saved in my factory except me. Can't you pray that I get saved, too?"

I replied, "Kneel with me right here." He knelt with me right there and the pastor and I prayed for him, and God saved his soul.

I began walking around the room again. I got right by the mayor, and the mayor looked up at me, and said, "Preacher I'm a good Methodist. No, I'm not a good Methodist. I'm a bad Methodist. Ask God to save me, too."

I answered, "Kneel with me right here." He knelt down with me. Pastor Johnson and I prayed for him, and God saved the mayor's soul.

When he arose from his knees, the mayor said, "We are going to have a parade in town; we are going to put a Bible in a float, the biggest float in the parade. We are going to ask everyone in town to come to your revival, and besides that, we are going to give you the keys to the city of Oskaloosa, Iowa."

So the city that tried to kick me out of town ended up being the city that gave me the keys to the city. I tell you, GOD CAN TURN THINGS AROUND.

- 72 -

Receiving a Tent on a Mountain

For several days at home in Richmond, Virginia, I had been praying for a large gospel tent. God seemed to speak to me that I should not expect Him to bring the tent into my living room, but I should get out on the road and begin looking for it. So I asked my son John Robert Ward, an Assemblies of God minister, to travel with me. He asked, "Where shall we go, since you want a tent as big as a football field?"

I answered, "There is a preacher in Cincinnati, Ohio, who is conducting a city-wide tent revival. Perhaps he has a tent for sale. Let us go there and see him."

So we embarked for Cincinnati. When we arrived, we got a motel room. I stayed in the room praying, and my son went to see the preacher. The evangelist said, "I don't want to sell my big tent, but I have a small tent which I will sell for seven thousand dollars. And I would rather bury it in the ground than sell it for a penny less than that."

In the meantime, at the motel, I could hear a man praying in the room next to ours. He was bombarding Heaven. He was praying with such fervency that I was getting anointed just listening to him. I felt that I had to go over and ask him to pray for us to find a tent. So I began to ask God to tell me something about the fellow. The Lord said, "He is a black preacher who needed an automobile, and when A.A. Allen was receiving an offering, he gave one hundred dollars, as a real sacrifice offering, and I gave him a new white Cadillac automobile."

Well, I got to shouting, because I had made a sacrifice to God that I might "make a covenant with God around a sacrifice offering," asking God for a large tent. It is not that I was going to "Buy" the tent with an offering. It is a covenant entered into with God that I would withhold nothing from Him in my earnest seeking after His will.

I waited a few minutes until the fellow next door had eased up in his prayer. Then I went over and knocked on his door. A woman opened the door. I said, "God told me that there is a preacher in this room, and that I should ask him to pray for me."

The fellow came around the corner of the room, saying, "I am a preacher."

I averred, "God told me that you were praying for a Cadillac, and gave A.A. Allen a hundred dollars as a sacrifice offering, and that God gave you a new, white Cadillac."

He replied, "That's exactly right, and there is my white Cadillac down there. I could not find any parking space near the room. So it is almost the length of the motel away."

I told him how my son and I were looking for a large gospel tent. He put his hand on my head, praying for me, and suddenly he began to prophesy, "Thus saith the Lord, thou shalt find the tent before midnight to night."

I was so thankful that God had put me in the room next to this preacher. What a blessing he was to me. I never saw him before nor since, but for an hour or so he was a great treasure to me.

When my son came back to the room, telling me that the preacher said that he would rather bury the tent than sell it for less than $7,000, and I did not have anything like that amount of money, I knew that was not the tent that God had for us. So exuberantly I began to tell my son that the preacher next door had prophesied that we would have the tent before midnight. All the time I am talking, I am packing my suitcase.

So my son asked, "What are we going to do now?"

I answered, "God told me to get out and look for the tent, saying, 'Seek and ye shall find.' "

Therefore, John and I prayed, "Dear Lord, we are asking for direction. We know not which way to go. Guide us in Thy perfect will."

When we finished praying, John asked, "Did God say anything to you?"

I smiled. "He said, 'Go south.' "

We got in our car, got on Highway 75, and headed south. Every hundred miles or so, my son would say, "How much farther south?"

I would reply, "Keep going."

Finally we entered the state of Alabama. We had left Cincinnati, Ohio. When we came to the small town of Fort Payne, Alabama, God said, "Go on top of that mountain."

I felt like we were at the end of the world. But we drove up the mountain, going around many curves. When we reached the top, we were flabbergasted. For sitting up there in the dark was a large tent, as big as a football field.

I said to John, "They will not mind if we just lift a side curtain, and look inside." It was about 11:30 P.M.

We lifted a side curtain and were even more astonished, because the tent was packed with seven thousand people, and the minister was still preaching. My son and I went inside and fortunately found two seats in the very back.

The preacher quit preaching at five or ten minutes to midnight. I told my son, "You run that way, and I will run this way, and whoever gets to the minister first, ask him if he has a tent to sell, because that preacher in Cincinnati prophesied that we would have the tent before midnight, and it is almost five minutes until twelve now."

My son, being younger, reached the preacher first. He asked, "Do you have a tent to sell?"

The preacher replied, "I have a big tent for you."

My son asked, "How much is it?"

The evangelist said, "Not one red cent. God just told me to give it to you."

Jubilant, John asked further, "How big is the tent?"

The preacher smiled, "It is the same size as this one. In fact, they are twin tents. It is as large as a football field." John looked at his watch, and it was a minute before midnight.

Suppose that we had stayed home, praying for the tent to come to us. It may never have come from Alabama to Virginia to find us. But God had put an automatic guidance system in us, and He had guided us as we journeyed. He could not have guided us if we had stayed home, sitting in the rocking chair, but God guides us while we are on the move for Him.

Several months later a businessman went to see the evangelist, and said, "I heard that you gave William A. Ward a large gospel tent, so I want to give you this twenty-five thousand dollars to buy you a new tent." You see, it is impossible to outgive God. The Lord will be debtor to no man. When you give to God, He gives back to you, and He has a bigger shovel than you have.

- 73 -

"Before Eleven O'Clock in the Morning"

On the last day of one of my revivals for Danny Davis in Bakersfield, California, he said, "I certainly need a new car."

I answered, "What kind of a car do you want?"

He replied, "I would like to show you the car. It is in the Pontiac showroom downtown."

I told him, "I leave first thing in the morning, but take me down there and let me see the car after church tonight."

It was about 11:00 P.M. when Danny Davis and I stood looking in the showroom window at the beautiful, new car. I said, "First thing in the morning, go in and get that car."

He answered, "It is impossible. I don't have the money to get that car."

I smiled, "You will have that car by eleven o'clock in the morning."

He said, "I have already tried to get it, and they will not sell it to me."

I repeated my assertion, "You will have the car by eleven A.M."

When I arrived back in Richmond, Virginia, Brother Davis called me, shouting over the telephone. "You were right! I have the car, and I got it before eleven o'clock in the morning!"

- 74 -

An Angel Rode in the Car with Me

I closed a revival in Saginaw, Michigan, and, as I got in my car to drive to Richmond after church, a woman ran out, and said, "Brother Ward, I see a big angel sitting in the front seat with you. He will protect you."

I had driven nearly two hundred miles, and it was midnight. The speed limit on the turnpike was sixty-five miles an hour, so I had the cruise control on sixty-five. I fell sound asleep at the wheel. It was my first trip in my new car, and the old devil was trying to wreck it and maybe kill me. Suddenly I awoke, as someone was shaking me violently. I was just going off the highway and headed for a drop of about twenty feet.

When I realized what was happening, I overcompensated, turned the wheel too much, and the car went from one side of the road to the other. Then it turned completely around, and I was headed back up the road from which I had come. I saw the cars coming toward me. They could have piled into me, but God gave them the presence of mind to slow down and then stop. I turned the car around and headed into Dayton, Ohio to get a motel and go to sleep.

I thanked God that an angel had really been riding with me, and I could definitely feel him shaking me to awaken me.

- 75 -

Thirty Ten Dollar Bills

Sister Stanley was a wonderful woman in our church in Richmond, Virginia. One day she came to me and said, "I am going to have to leave the church, because God told me to start my own church."

I went into a church room and began to pray, "Dear God, what am I going to do? You know that Sister Stanley tithes ten dollars every Sunday, and we are just making it now. What are we going to do without her ten dollars each week?"

God spoke to me, saying, "You will never miss her ten dollars." Immediately I felt better.

Next Sunday, Sister Stanley was gone, but I noticed that a new man whom I had never seen was present in the service. The man in charge of taking up the offering came to me after church, and said, "The new man in church is Mr. Cox, and he put thirty ten dollar bills in the offering plate."

That Brother Cox came to church for years after that. He gave thirty $10 bills for several Sundays. Then he dropped down to twenty $10 bills. And after a while he dropped down to ten $10 bills every Sunday. He never gave anything but $10 bills, and I think the lowest that he ever gave was three tens.

God showed me that He could take care of His church. It was only a few weeks after Sister Stanley left that forty-three people came and joined our church the same night. They said, "We are all tithe-payers, and we have been worshiping in a home. But God told us to come join your church."

I had to ask God to forgive me for thinking that His church was apt to go under because of the absence of one wonderful woman, whom He had called to start her own church.

- 76 -

Meeting a Friend at the Garden Tomb in Jerusalem

In 1950 I was in Jerusalem. When I awoke one morning God told me that as I would enter the resurrection tomb of Jesus that day, I would bump into a wonderful friend of mine from America that I did not know was in Jerusalem. He said that my friend would be coming out of the tomb as I was entering it. I told several people what God had said to me, and I asked, "I wonder who I am going to bump into as I enter the resurrection tomb?"

As I entered the tomb, a man bumped into me, saw who I was, and said, "Bill, what are you doing here?" I was astonished to see that it was Dr. Jonas E. Miller. He and I had pastored the Calvary Gospel Church in Washington, D.C., together for several years. He did not know that I was in Jerusalem, and I did not know that he was there either. But God knew that we were both there; and He saw to it that we met at the resurrection tomb.

In a few days it was Easter Sunday. For the first time they were having a resurrection service at the Garden Tomb for the public, and I was asked to be the speaker. So I preached on the resurrection of Christ, standing near the doorway to the empty tomb. Remember that this was 1950, and Israel had become a nation again only two years earlier in 1948.

- 77 -

God Directs Our Paths

It is wonderful that God knows where we are at all times. One day in Richmond, I was talking to the Lord. I was saying how I would like to see Brother Roberts, a preacher friend of mine, but I had no idea where he was in the world.

God told me that my friend happened to be in Richmond and that he would be crossing the street at Sixth and Broad at 3:00 that afternoon. The Lord said, "You stand under that big clock on the building at three o'clock, and your friend will walk across the street right to you."

So I was standing under the clock at 3:00 P.M. and my friend, Brother Roberts, came walking across the street. He said, "Brother Ward, I had no idea where you were. What are you doing here?"

I answered, "Waiting for you." God is interested in each detail of our lives.

I know that many people cannot understand these things. They think that we are probably crazy. But when you talk to God, you know that He knows all things, and He can reveal things to us so easily. Thank God for who He is and what He means to our lives.

- 78 -

A Young Was Man Struck by a Golf Ball

Brother Heflin and I were playing golf one day. A young man was hit at close range by a golf ball, striking him in the temple at a terrific rate of speed. He was stretched out on the ground unconscious.

One young man said, "I don't think that he is breathing."

Another man cried, "How can we call an ambulance?"

Brother Heflin and I arrived at that moment, and Brother Heflin said, "Don't you men worry about anything. We are preachers, and we pray for the sick. Everything is going to be all right." So Brother Heflin and I began praying out loud for that boy.

As we prayed, he opened his eyes. They asked him where he hurt. He answered, "I don't hurt any place." He got up.

They declared, "We will take you either to the hospital or to your home."

He answered, "I feel fine, and I want to continue playing golf." And he did.

- 79 -

My Revival on a Greyhound Bus

In May of 1942, I was in Washington, D.C., and God called me to conduct a revival meeting in

Bartlesville, Oklahoma. I had a Packard automobile at the time, and I put my things in it and was just driving out of Washington, D.C., on my way to Oklahoma when God spoke to me and said, "You are not to go in the car."

I turned around, went home, and took a taxicab down to the railroad station and was just buying my ticket on the train when God spoke to me and said, "You are not to go on the train."

So I got a taxicab and went over to the National Airport and was just about to purchase my ticket on the airplane when God spoke to me and said, "You are not to go on the plane."

I answered, "Dear Lord, please don't make me hitchhike."

God spoke to me and said, "Go on the Greyhound bus."

So I bought my ticket on the bus and was traveling through the countryside that night. From 7:00 until 9:00 the people on that bus were singing one worldly song after another. They sang, "The music comes in, goes around and comes out here and there" or somewhere. They sang all kinds of worldly songs until I got so sick of them that it seemed I couldn't stand it any longer.

So I began to pray, "Oh, God, closet me in with Thee. Help me to get in the basket and pull the lid down and shut myself in with God and get away from this atmosphere and forget who I am and where I am and just enjoy the fellowship of God."

As I began to talk to the Lord, He was talking to

me, and I forgot where I was. All of a sudden I awoke to the realization that I had shouted almost at the top of my voice, "Well, hallelujah!"

I heard a fellow at the back of the bus say, "My God, there is a preacher on board."

A drunken sailor came up the aisle to me and said, "You are a preacher, aren't you?"

I answered, "Yes."

He confirmed, "I am drunk, and I am on my way home to see my wife and three children. I have a three-day leave from the Naval Training Station in Norfolk, Virginia, and when I get home I will be so drunk that they will have to put me to bed, and I will never remember seeing my wife and children. I will break their hearts. Preacher, won't you pray that God will sober me up, that I won't drink any more?"

I said, "You kneel with me right here in the aisle and we will pray together." So he and I prayed, and I watched God as He sobered him up and saved him.

Then he said, "Preacher, stay right here." He went to the back of the bus and, one after another, he brought four drunken sailors up to me. I prayed with each one of them until I felt God had saved them. Then they each became my evangelists and they went all through the bus speaking to people about their souls and bringing people to me for prayer.

Finally, the bus driver turned and said, "Preacher, I have been driving a bus for eighteen years. I have had all kinds of things happen on my bus, but this is the first time that I have ever had an old-fashioned revival meeting on my bus." He said, "I wish you would come up and pray for me, too."

So I went up and prayed for the driver, and to make a long story shorter, nine people were converted on that Greyhound bus traveling through the night. Then the people began to sing again, but now they were singing, "I Come to the Garden Alone," and "Jesus, Lover of my Soul," and "At the Cross, At the Cross," and "There Is a Fountain."

I have been preaching for more than sixty years, but the greatest revival I have ever had was on a Greyhound Bus traveling through the night. It was all because I got alone with God and shut out everything and everybody, and in the solitude with my Savior I cried out, "Hallelujah!"

- 80 -

"I Don't Ever Want to See Your Face Again"

Once, when my wife was working, I stopped my car downtown to let my wife out. A policeman gave me a ticket for double parking. I said, "I am not double parked; I am simply letting my wife out of the car."

Since I felt that I had been given the ticket unfairly, I went to court to contest the ticket. I got there when the court opened at 9:00 A.M. and sat there until 5:00 P.M. I was the only person still in the courtroom. The judge said, "Is there anyone whose case has not been heard?"

I answered, "Yes, your Honor," and walked up to the bench.

The judge asked, "Who are you?"

I replied, "I am a preacher."

He got red in the face and said, "I hate preachers." He continued, "Give me your ticket. I will dismiss your case, but I don't ever want to see your face again." He got up from the bench, and I watched him walk over to the door and go out of the room.

He never had to look at my face again, but I had to look at his. The next morning, I opened my newspaper, and there was the judge's face, taking up a quarter of the front page. The writing underneath his face read, "Yesterday, the judge closed his court, walked over to the door, went through the door, and dropped dead."

All that I could think of were the words: "I hate preachers." "I don't ever want to see your face again."

- 81 -

"You Will Receive a Nasty Letter Every Day"

When I pastored the church in Richmond, I was on the radio three times a day and on television twice a week. I was telling the people that Jesus heals the sick. One morning my wife and I went to the Post

Office to get the mail, and there was an exceedingly nasty letter in my P.O. Box. I would not have thought so much about it, except whoever sent the letter claimed, "From now on, you will get a nasty letter from me every day of your life." That was too much for me. Of course, the writer did not have the courage to sign the letter.

My wife and I stopped in front of the post office and I prayed, "Dear Lord, show me who wrote this letter, so that I will not have to receive another one like it every day the rest of my life."

The Lord answered. "The man who wrote the letter is named Jones, and he has a shoe repair place right around the corner from the post office."

Within five minutes of the time we received the letter, I was standing in Mr. Jones' place of business. He said, "What can I do for you?"

I answered, "You can stop sending me these nasty letters."

He cried, "Who are you?"

I replied, "I am William A. Ward, and here is the letter that I just got from you."

He ran over and locked his front door, so that no customers could enter. He screamed, "How did you know that I wrote that letter? I did not sign it."

I declared, "The same God who heals the sick, told me that you wrote that letter."

Flabbergasted, he asked, "Please forgive me. God must be with you. I will never write you a letter like that again. Will you forgive me?"

I answered, "I forgive you, but I must tell you that

if you want to continue your business, you will have to get another building, because as I walked through the front door, God spoke to me and said that this building will be torn down within two weeks."

I went by that place of business a couple of days after two weeks. It had been torn completely down, and there was nothing but a flat piece of ground.

- 82 -

Knowing Things by the Holy Ghost

I was riding in a car returning to Zion Bible College in East Providence, Rhode Island, from Washington, D.C. It was loaded with students. We were passing through a city in New Jersey, and one student kept saying, "I wish that I knew where this preacher lives. I would like to see him."

The other students chimed in, "Yes, we wish that we could locate him."

Finally I said, "Well, I can find him for you, if it is that important."

The students laughed, saying, "Why, you don't even know him, how could you find his house?"

I prayed to God to show me where he lived. I would say, "Turn here, go down this street." In a matter of minutes, I said, "He lives in that house on the corner."

Everyone laughed, "We know that he does not live there. Why don't you go and knock on the door?"

I answered, "I am not the one who wants to see him. You want to see him. You knock on the door."

One fellow got out of the car and knocked on the door.

The preacher came to the door and invited us all in. We went in and visited with him for about a half an hour. The preacher kept saying, "How did you find my house? I recently moved here, and I didn't think anyone knew my address yet."

We all shouted, "Well, God knows where you live!"

- 83 -

A Boy Comes Home

In Cincinnati, a woman came to me, saying, "Tomorrow my husband is going to quit his job, and he and I are going all over America in search of our son. He left home more than a year ago, and he has not been back. We miss him so much that we are going to seek for him."

I answered, "Sister, do not let your husband quit his job, and do not go searching for your son. We are going to command him to come home in the name of Jesus."

After prayer, I told her, "Your son will come home tomorrow evening at five. He will say, 'Mom, I am hungry. Do you have anything to eat?' You will say, 'I have prepared your favorite dinner, and it is ready to put on the table.'

"After dinner, he will say, 'Mom, I want to move back home,' and you will have cleaned his room, and say, 'Everything is ready, move in now.' "

That night, the mother came to church, praising God. She told me the story, and said, "Everything came out just as you said that it would, and my son is in his room right now."

- 84 -

"Look At That Piece of Junk He Is Driving"

I was driving to Calvary Pentecostal Camp in my Chevrolet station wagon God had given to me about nine years earlier. I loved it, because God gave it to me.

When I drove on the camp, I heard one boy say to another boy, "Brother Ward prays everyone into a new car, and look at that piece of junk he is driving."

That just about floored me because I always thought of that station wagon as a miracle car that God gave to me. It never occurred to me that it looked like junk. I forgot that it had been nine years since God had given it to me and it still hurt me that anyone would think that something that God gave me was just a piece of junk.

However, I saw right there that I had to believe God for a better car. I walked across the field from where I had parked my car, and I said, "Now, God, I probably wouldn't be trusting you for a new car if I hadn't heard those boys say that, but since they did say it, I claim a new car."

As I reached the platform, Brother Heflin was taking up pledges and asking those who would like to pledge $100 for the camp to stand at the front of the Tabernacle. I went down, and while I was standing there pledging $100, a woman tapped me on the shoulder, and said, "I'm giving you five thousand dollars on a new car."

It was the same night, and not over thirty minutes after I declared, "I am trusting You, dear God, for a new car."

That is why if anybody says, "God doesn't work miracles," you have come too late to influence me. Thank You, Jesus!

Within one week, without any offering being taken for the new car, I had a total of $11,000 handed to me, and a man who had a Lincoln Town Car for sale for $14,950 said to me, "You can have it for eleven thousand dollars."

- 85 -

God Can Heal Broken Elevators

In 1940, I was holding a revival meeting in San Francisco, and I got the nastiest letter in the mail. It said, "You are a charlatan. You are telling people on the radio every day that Jesus heals, and everybody knows that the days of miracles are over."

As I read that letter, I felt smaller and smaller. I don't know why we take those letters we don't like and stick them right over our hearts, but I did. I put it in my inside coat pocket.

The next day I was riding in an elevator in a tall building in San Francisco. There was just one lady and myself on the elevator, and the elevator broke down between floors.

That lady went all to pieces and began to scream, "My God, we are going to die! The elevator is going to fall to the basement, and we are going to be killed!"

I prayed, "God, there must be some reason why I am stuck on this elevator with this woman."

And the Lord answered, "Yes, there is a reason. She is the woman who wrote you that nasty letter that you have in your pocket."

I turned to her, and I said, "Sister, quit screaming a minute. I want to talk to you. I am William A. Ward, and yesterday I received a letter from you, stating that the days of miracles are over, and anyone who believes in miracles is a charlatan."

She said, "My God, how did you know that I wrote you that letter?"

I replied, "Because the same God that works miracles can also speak. He is a speaking God. He told me that you wrote the letter."

She screamed, "It doesn't matter anyway because we are both going to be killed!"

I asked, "What floor do you want to reach?"

She told me, and I declared, "All right, the elevator is going to work now, since God let me talk to you."

I pressed the button, and the elevator took off and went directly to her floor.

As she got out, she said, "Preacher, pray for me. I have made the mistake of my life. God still works miracles, and the God who heals the sick can even heal elevators."

My self-esteem went up about five degrees. I realized that I was not a charlatan, and I knew that I was charged with God's power. God had spoken to me, and God was working through me.

- 86 -

A New Car, the First Thing in the Morning

I was conducting a revival in Dallas, Texas, for W.V. Grant, Sr. One night in the middle of my sermon, I walked over, put my hand on the head of Mrs. Sue Patterson, the piano player, and prayed God to give her a new car.

The very next day, I was studying, and someone knocked on my door, saying, "The piano player wants you to come see her new car. It is parked in front of the church."

I went out quickly and rejoiced to see the beautiful new car that she had. She said that someone had awakened her at eight o'clock that morning to take her down and get her a new automobile. Praise the Lord!

- 87 -

A Man Was Going to Commit Suicide in Las Vegas

I was home in Richmond, Virginia, and a man called me on the telephone from Connecticut. He said, "I have to tell you my story. I have just returned from Las Vegas, Nevada. One night there, I determined that I would commit suicide, because I had lost two hundred thousand dollars at the gambling tables.

As I put the gun to my head to blow my brains out, my eyes fell on your book, *How To Be Successful*, which I had purchased in the book store that day. I laid the gun down and began to read the book. I read it all night long, and in the morning I gave my heart to God and had no more desire to end my life.

"God used your book to save my life. I have told my story to a millionaire, and we have decided to offer you two million dollars a year to travel across America and lecture on 'How to be successful.' "

I responded, "I am a preacher, and I would not give up preaching to lecture."

The next night he called me back, and said, "I have told Rev. Norman Vincent Peale about your book, and he wants two hundred books to give out in his church in New York City."

I sent the two hundred books.

A week or two later I was preaching in Norfolk, Virginia. The pastor invited me for dinner. He affirmed, "Before we eat, let us watch Norman Vincent Peale on television." Imagine my surprise when Rev. Peale showed my book on television, and took up the entire half hour telecast talking very favorably about the book.

- 88 -

My Son Was Kneeling on the Ball

My oldest son, John, when he was about seven years old, was playing with a softball in the field across the street from our home in Tulsa, Oklahoma. The grass was more than knee high. Soon he threw his ball in the air, and when it came down, he could not find it. It was lost in the high grass. He spent quite a while hunting for the ball.

Finally he cried to me, "Dad, I can't find my ball. Please pray that the Lord will let me find it." So I prayed out loud. In a minute, my son dropped on his knees to continue praying, and he thought that he must be kneeling on a rock, because it was uncomfortable. He reached down to move the rock and found his ball. He had been kneeling on the ball. That was the way that God allowed my son to find his ball quickly.

- 89 -

Finding Where I Was Staying in Rome, Italy

In 1950, I was in Rome, Italy. From the airport, I was taken to the Pentecostal church, where the pastor had been put in jail twenty-two times for preaching the gospel. I preached in the Sunday morning service, and after church they took me to a parishioner's home where I was to spend the night.

I asked the folks to give me a note stating the address of the house, so that I could give it to a streetcar conductor or a bus driver. I was in a hurry to go to the Vatican and see the Pope.

They wrote the address of the house in Italian. I could not read it, but I gave it to about four streetcar conductors and three bus drivers, and they all let me ride to the end of the line. They probably called out the street where I should have gotten off, but I did not understand them. Each time I rode back to the center of town and started over.

By now it was getting late, about 11:00 P.M., so in desperation I prayed, "God, You show me how to get to the house where I am staying."

I rode on a streetcar until the Lord said, "Get off here." I got off the streetcar, and God guided me down this street and up this avenue. Finally the Lord said, "This is the street where you are staying."

I looked, but it was a very long street, and the houses were all row houses, joined together, and they all looked alike. I said, "Dear God, You will have to show me which one of these houses is the right one."

The Lord led me to a house in the middle of the block and said, "This is the house."

It was midnight when I knocked on the door. The people were so glad to see me. I suppose they had worried over me. They said things to me which I could not understand and sat me down at the dining room table. They put a big bowl of spaghetti on the table. I thought that this was the entire meal, so I filled up on the spaghetti. It turned out to be a sixteen-course meal that they were serving, but I was completely full of spaghetti.

I wanted to tell them that I had just experienced one of the greatest miracles of my life in being divinely directed to their house, but I could not speak Italian, and they could not speak English. All that I knew about them was that they loved the Lord with all their hearts, and all they knew about me was that I loved the Lord, too.

- 90 -

Three Doctors Could Not Find Her Gall Bladder

A doctor in Richlands, Virginia, asked me to come to the hospital and pray for his patients. The first woman we prayed for had one hundred and fifty gallstones, and her gall bladder was diseased. He declared, "At eleven o'clock tomorrow morning, we are going to take her gall bladder out. Please pray for her."

I had just come from Sister Campbell's house. I remember that I had prayed for her more than eighteen years earlier, when she had terrible heart trouble. I had prayed for God to give her a heart transplant. They had an appointment to take her to Bluefield to the hospital. The doctor told her, "Why, Mrs. Campbell, you have a brand new heart. We don't understand this at all." Through the last twenty years, her heart has been perfect.

As I was remembering Sister Campbell, I prayed, "Dear Lord, give this woman a gall bladder transplant. Take this old gall bladder with its one hundred and fifty gallstones and give her a new gall bladder, which is perfect."

The next morning at 11:00, they operated on the woman and could not find her gall bladder. They called in different doctors. Each one saying, "Maybe the gall bladder is here or there," but no doctor could find her gall bladder. So they sewed her back up and sent her home. She did so well at home that she did not return to the hospital.

Three months went by, and they asked her to come to the hospital. They promised not to operate on her. They just wanted to see if they could find her gall bladder. When they x-rayed her, her gall bladder showed up immediately, but the doctors noticed that it was a brand new, perfect gall bladder, and there were no gallstones.

God had given her a gall bladder transplant, and I believe that He would not let the doctors find her gall bladder, because He did not want them to cut out what He had just put in her body.

I must reiterate that I am no healer. I could not heal anybody. I do not believe that any person can heal anyone. I simply believe that God is the Healer. He made the body in the first place, and He can heal it if it goes bad. If anyone is healed, we are jealous to see that God gets all the glory. He, and He alone, is the miracle worker.

- 91 -

A Thousand Dollars Came in the Mail

One night in my revival in Fayetteville, North Carolina, the offering was very small, and I said to the people, "Don't worry about it. I will get a thousand dollars in the mail tomorrow."

After I said that, I thought, "Perhaps I should have said, 'I might get' or 'I could get.' " Then I thought, "Maybe I was prophesying, and I didn't know it."

It must have been God speaking through me, for the next day, I received a letter from Mrs. Bow in Roanoke, Virginia, and it had $1,000 in it for my ministry. It had to have been mailed before I said that I would get it.

- 92 -

The Second Mortgage Is Paid

The next morning I would have to leave early and fly from Richmond to West Texas, where I was to preach in the West Texas Businessmen's Convention. About 9:00 P.M. the man who held a second mortgage on our house called and said, "I need money now, and you owe me $1,430. So bring it over to me."

I said, "I have to leave first thing in the morning for Texas. I will only be gone a week. When I return, I will bring you the $1,430."

He said, "You are not going to Texas owing me this money. I need it now."

When I hung up the phone, I only had a moment to feel bad, and then I felt worse, for my wife came to me, and said, "You cannot go to Texas and leave all that wood in the den. Spiders are breeding there."

What had happened was that my wife had been in charge of tearing down Ginter's Mansion, said to be the second most beautiful house east of the Mississippi River. And I had purchased some beautiful cherry wood from the house. I had nowhere to store the wood, so I just filled our den with it. Now my wife was saying that I had to get that wood out of the den before I left town.

I knew that I had to be on that airplane in the morning, for I was scheduled to preach the convention in Texas. I dropped down on my knees and did as Rev. R.W. Schambach had told me. He said when you get in trouble, just look up to God, and cry, "HELP!"

I had no sooner yelled "HELP!" to God than the telephone rang. A man said, "I will give you $1,430 for the wood that you have in the den."

I cried, "Sold!" I said it so fast that it scared him, and he began to back off.

He said, "Wait a minute. I thought that the wood was worth more than two thousand dollars."

I answered, "It is, but when I have been praying God to send me $1,430, and you offer me exactly $1,430, I have to know that God is in it. There is one important problem involved. My wife says that I have to get the wood out of our den before I leave for Texas, and I am leaving first thing in the morning."

He answered, "I am bringing you a check for $1,430 right now, and don't worry about the wood. I need it tomorrow for the house I am building. I have a crew of men. We will be there first thing in the morning and move all that wood out of your house. We have trucks and everything."

In fifteen or twenty minutes he was at our house with a check. I rushed it over to the second mortgage man. He said, "I thought that you did not have the money tonight. Where did you get the money so fast?"

I replied, "God sent it," and indeed He did.

Early in the morning the fellow was there with his men, and got all of the wood out of our house, and even swept the den clean. I left for Texas in total

even swept the den clean. I left for Texas in total victory: the second mortgage paid and the wood out of the den. Hallelujah!

- 93 -

Bob Hope Told Sid Solomon to Get My Book

Not long after my book *How to Be Successful* was published, I was driving through Arizona late at night. I was discouraged over the book and began to feel that hardly anybody would ever hear about it.

Suddenly I felt to turn the car radio on. Bob Hope was speaking to Sid Solomon on a coast-to-coast program. Mr. Solomon was the manager of the St. Louis Blues hockey team. The team was playing for the World Cup, and Bob Hope was a part owner of the club.

Mr. Hope told Sid Solomon that he should buy copies of my book, *How To Be Successful*, and give one to every member of the St. Louis Blues hockey team so that they could be successful in playing for the World Cup. Sid Solomon said, "I already bought thirty-five copies and have given one to each member of the team."

And he had, for Mr. Solomon had written to me, stating that he had purchased a copy of my book, and he liked it so much that he wanted to give a copy to each member of his St. Louis Blues hockey team. I wish that I could say that the hockey club won the World Cup, but the truth is that they lost the match.

Others began to hear about the book, and soon I received a phone call from Austin, Texas. It told me of a conference on success in Austin, in which the six thousand people who had attended voted my book, *How To Be Successful,* as the best in America on success.

- 94 -

"That Lady Who Was Paralyzed Is Healed"

I prayed one Friday night for a woman who was totally paralyzed. They brought her from the hospital to our revival meeting in an ambulance and brought her down the aisle on a rolling bed. We prayed for her that night, but nothing happened. She was not healed. The same ambulance that brought her to church took her back to the hospital.

Sunday night, as I was getting ready to preach, a woman hurried down the aisle. She was so excited, crying, "Wait a minute preacher! I want to tell you something. I have just come from the hospital, and that lady who was paralyzed, that you prayed for Friday, is healed. She is walking all around the hospital and is getting ready to come to church tonight."

- 95 -

Paralyzed Woman Healed Over Period of Months

God is the Healer, and He has healed thousands and thousands of times. He does not have to heal the same way every time.

In 1951, in Roswell, New Mexico, there was a paralyzed woman lying on a bed in the center aisle of our huge gospel tent. I went down and prayed for her. She did not seem to be healed, but a couple of weeks later someone came to the tent and told me, "That lady who was totally paralyzed, and was lying on the bed in the center aisle of the tent, is getting better. She is being healed."

Then I learned a year later that she was up and walking around, completely healed. Her full healing had taken perhaps six or seven months or more, but I am sure that she felt that it was worth waiting for the full recovery to be realized.

- 96 -

God Uses a Man From the Insane Asylum

During my revival with Pastor Bill Bishop in Saginaw, Michigan, a very dear lady who worked in an asylum for the mentally unbalanced got permission to bring eleven patients to the meeting one night. All eleven were healed by the power of God.

Before I prayed for them, I was taking pledges for the meetings, and one of the men that she had brought came to the front asking for a pledge. I offered him a $33 pledge, but he said, “Not that one.”

I offered him a $77 pledge, but he quickly stated, “Not that one.”

Then I presented him with a $100 pledge, but he again answered, “Not that one.”

I then gave him a $300 pledge, but he averred, “Not that one.”

I found him a $500 pledge, but he shook his head, saying, “Not that one.”

All that I had left was a $1,000 pledge, and when he saw it, he took it, crying, “That is the one.”

When the man returned to his seat, the lady who had brought him, reached forward, saying, “What pledge did you get?” He showed her, and she said, “Give that pledge to me; I want to pay it for you.”

After church she came up and paid the pledge. The miracle was that we were behind on paying the bills of the revival, and I had been praying before church, “Dear Lord, let someone take a one thousand dollar ledge and pay it tonight, so that we can get these bills paid.” And God used a man who had been in a mental institution for years to help get the bills paid.

- 97 -

New York City Miracles

In 1940, as far as I know, Billy Graham and I were the only preachers to preach in the San Francisco World Fair and also in the New York World Fair that same year. In New York, I often preached in the World Fair in the daytime and in my revival at the Russian Pentecostal Church at night. At that time, I think that the church was on West 6th Street, and I preached there every night for five weeks.

In one night's service alone, God healed about thirty people of tremendous afflictions. In that meeting, a totally deaf man was healed. After church, while walking with his wife on the way to their car, a truck had to come to an abrupt stop at the corner. The man jumped two or three feet. His wife asked him what was the matter. He answered that it was the first time that he had ever heard tires screech against the pavement, when the truck driver applied the brakes, and he thought that the world had come to an end.

In that same meeting, a blind girl was healed. Also, a man who had a tumor as big as a grapefruit was healed. I asked him to go to the hospital and have an x-ray made. He did; the tumor had shrunk to the size of a pea, and the following day the x-ray showed that it was gone altogether.

That same night a woman brought her daughter to church who was twenty-four years old. For twenty-one years, since she was three years of age, she had been deaf and dumb, had never spoken a word and never heard a sound. I prayed for her and said, "There is a word that I want you to say, and I want you to turn around and say it to these fifteen hundred people now."

She turned and said loudly, "JESUS."

I said, "Say it again."

She cried, "JESUS."

Then I affirmed, "There is a word that your mother has waited twenty-one years to hear you say, and I want you to turn to her, and say it now."

She faced her mother and cried, "MAMA!"

I said, "Say it again!"

And she cried, "MAMA!"

Her mother broke and they fell into each other's arms, and their tears mingled. The girl was totally healed.

So many people were being healed that a man asked me, "Will you please not go home yet preacher? I want to get my mother. She is paralyzed and has not been able to flex a finger or move a toe. Moreover, she has not been able to turn over in bed in five years. She lives on the fifth floor, and there is no elevator in that building. I have to get somebody to help me carry her down the five flights of stairs and bring her to the church. It might take me an hour, so would you stay here until I get back?"

I answered, "I will stay."

It was little more than an hour when he came back. He and another man carried his mother up the church steps. They had a rolling bed and rolled her up to the platform. God instantly healed her. She later told me that when she got home, she walked up the five flights of steps. And every night, the rest of that revival, she would walk down the five flights of steps, come to church, and after church, she would walk up the five flights of steps, for God had completely healed her.

- 98 -

God Works at Both Ends of the Tent

In Roswell, New Mexico, I was praying for a blind woman on the platform at the front of the tent. Unbeknownst to me, there was a blind woman sitting in the very back of the tent, which seemed like a block away. The woman in the back prayed, "Dear Lord, while you heal that woman in the front of the tent, you can also heal me here in the back of the tent."

The woman in the front of the tent began to shout, "Praise God! I am healed! I can see!"

When she did, the lady in the back of the tent stood up, and shouted, "Praise God! I am healed, too! I can see, too!"

Then she told the audience that she had been plagued with the very same trouble of blindness. She had told the Lord she could not get to me in the front of the tent to be prayed for, but had asked Him to heal her in the back of the tent without anyone praying for her. At the same time as the lady on the platform was healed with someone praying for her, this lady received, too.

We have found that God is able and willing to heal all people who have faith, for faith is the currency of Heaven.

- 99 -

I Am Afraid of Dignified People

While I was at Rev. Augut's church in Taunton, Massachusetts, God told me one night in the middle of my sermon to go over to Mrs. Augut, sitting on a front seat, and pray for her. As I preached, I walked over to Mrs. Augut. I was just about to lay my hand on her head, but she looked at me in such a dignified way that I immediately lost all my courage, and took my upraised hand and, with it, began to scratch the back of my head. I then walked as I preached to the other side of the church.

Again God said, "Go lay your hand on her head and pray for her." So I walked back over, stood in front of her, and raised my hand. But just then, she looked full into my eyes in that dignified way, and, again, I scratched the back of my head, walking back to the other side of the church. Once more God said, "Go pray for Mrs. Augut." The third time I walked over to her. This time, even though I was still preaching, I closed my eyes so that if she looked at me, I could not see her. I put my hand on her head and prayed out loud for her to be completely healed. Well I didn't even know that she was sick. I was surprised at my own prayer.

The power of God hit her, and she came out of that seat like an electric dynamo had struck her. She began to shout, "I am healed! I am healed!" Then she said, "I don't want to disturb Brother Ward's sermon, but I must tell you that I went to see Dr. Murphy today, a Catholic doctor here in town. He told me that I have 69 per cent sugar, sugar diabetes in the last stages. He said that I did not have six months to live. I have been sitting here, asking God how I could tell my husband that I only had six months to live, but I felt God heal me. I know that I am healed."

The next day Mrs. Augut went back to see Dr. Murphy. He affirmed, "I cannot understand it. A miracle has happened. Yesterday you had 69 per cent sugar, but today you are absolutely normal."

- 100 -

"You Will Be Blind in About Six Months"

When I was eighteen years old and attending Bible college in East Providence, Rhode Island, my eyes hurt me so much that I went to an eye specialist in Providence. He told me that the muscles to my short vision had been terribly overworked, while the muscles to my long vision had been grossly neglected. He said, "You will never be able to read another book as long as you live, and the only hope for you at this time is to go to a place like Arizona and stare off into the distance, for you will be blind within six months." Needless to say, I went to prayer for my eyes, but I was in school, and I did not stop reading.

Later, when I was writing my Ph.D. dissertation at the University of Texas, I read approximately three thousand books. After I got out of school, for many years I tried to read four books a day. And I have never again had trouble with my eyes since that day I prayed desperately about them.

- 101 -

My Wife Gets a New Automobile

When my wife heard that the piano player at Brother Grant's church had received a new car, she came to me with big tears flowing down her cheeks, saying, "If thou be a prophet of God, pray for me to get a new car, too." At first, I thought that she was kidding, but then I saw that she really meant business. So I laid my hand on her head and asked God to give her a new car.

I asked my wife, "What kind of car do you want?"

She replied, "A Pinto station wagon."

I asked, "What color?"

She answered, "Blue."

I continued, "What do you want on it?"

She declared, "Air conditioning and a heater."

Then I told my wife to dress as one who would get a new car that very day. She said, "Please don't hold cake and ice cream in front of me, and then let me be disappointed."

I said, "You want a new car; let us go get it."

She answered, "But, I know that we are broke. We have no money for a car."

We got in my car to go get a car for her. While we were driving, God told me to go by the post office and see what kind of mail that we might have in our P.O. box. I parked in front of the post office. There was only one letter in our box, and it had a check for $1,000 in it. A note in the letter said, "Use this check any way that you see fit."

That was good enough for me. I tried not to smile when I came out to the car, but I guess that I could not help it. My wife said, "Who did you see in the post office that you have come out with your face wreathed in smiles?"

I was mean, for I did not tell my wife that I had just been given $1,000. I drove to Universal Ford and asked the head salesman if they had a new Pinto in stock. He replied, "We have just one."

I asked, "What color is it?"

He answered, "Blue."

I asked, "Does it have air conditioning and a heater?"

He smiled, "Of course, and a radio, too."

I asked my wife to look at it and see if that was the car that she wanted. She saw the car and said, "This is exactly the car that I want."

I told the salesman, "Oil and grease it, and whatever else you do to prepare it, for she wants to drive it home."

That was the first car that my wife could call her very own, and she has always had her own car since that day. She has had six cars, and today, she has a Lincoln Town Car just like mine.

- 102 -

I Get a Three-layer Chocolate Cake

Over in China, a preacher came to me, saying, "I notice that if you say that you want anything, it is just a day or two, and you have it."

I smiled and answered, "If that is true, I want a three-layer chocolate cake."

The preacher began to laugh, and said, "That is one thing that you will not get, because there is not a three-layer chocolate cake in the entire country of China."

But, I think that it was two days later, when the preacher came into my hotel room, crying, "Come quick, Dr. Ward, and see the three-layer chocolate cake that somebody has baked for you."

It was such a beautiful and delicious cake, and I suppose all of the people with us on the preaching tour enjoyed at least one piece of it.

- 103 -

Receiving a New, Four-Bedroom Brick Home

I was conducting a revival in West Point, Virginia. A dear lady came to me, as I was praying for different people to receive a new car. She said, "I do not want a car. I need a new house. I have four children, and at this time, we are forced to live with my mother."

I asked, "What kind of house do you want?"

She replied, "A four-bedroom house."

I asked, "Do you want a one-story house or a two-story house?"

She answered, "A two-story."

I continued, "A brick home or a wooden one?"

She said, "A brick house."

I declared, "You will have the house within thirty days."

She told me about thirty days later, "You should see the beautiful four-bedroom, brick, two-story home that God has given me, and it was free."

- 104 -

He Did Not Need the Special Shoe Any Longer

A man in Charlotte, North Carolina, was healed of a short leg. One leg was eleven inches shorter than the other, and he had a special shoe with an eleven inch sole on it. When God healed him in my revival meeting at the Garr Auditorium, people told me that the fellow went all over town, ringing doorbells, and telling folks that God had healed him and showing them the special shoe that he had worn for many years.

- 105 -

God Healed My Broken Automobile

I left Richmond, Virginia, to drive almost eight hundred miles to Grand Rapids, Michigan, to start a revival on Easter Sunday in 1994. When I had driven a little over two hundred miles, my car broke down. I could not drive it, and the garage people told me that I would have to leave my car in the garage all day, and perhaps I could drive the next morning.

I replied, "No, for I have to start the revival tomorrow morning." So, I laid hands on the car, praying, "Dear Lord, just as You can heal sick bodies, You can heal broken automobiles. I am going to drive this car to Michigan, and I command it to run beautifully until I get to Michigan, in the Name of Jesus."

I drove the car into Grand Rapids and started my revival the next morning on schedule. The car ran well all during my stay in Michigan. Then when my meetings were ended, I started driving it back to Virginia. I had gone a little over two hundred miles when, suddenly, the car broke down as it had done before.

Out on the Ohio Turnpike, I said, "Devil, you are really trying yourself. You never learn, do you?" Then I prayed, "Father, in the Name of Jesus, I command this car to run and carry me home." I began driving the car and arrived safely at home, driving a total of almost eight hundred miles that day as I had done going to Michigan. The car was completely healed and caused me no more trouble.

- 106 -

Three Hundred Dollars Was Given to Me in Jerusalem

My nephew, the late Dr. Wallace H. Heflin, Jr. had rented the largest auditorium in Jerusalem for a revival meeting. He had asked me to preach several services. I needed $300 desperately to pay bills that were due at home in Virginia. As always, I told absolutely nobody that I needed the money. Before I preached, I asked God for the money.

After the service, I was walking out of the building, and a man came to me, handing me exactly $300. I continued walking to the place where I could send the money home. Within a couple of hours of my prayer to God for the money, it was on its way to America, about eight thousand miles away.

- 107 -

About to Go over the Falls in a Canoe

When I was about fifteen years old, we were attending the Potomac Park Campground in Falling Waters, West Virginia. One day, I and Richard Bishop, perhaps a year younger than I was, and who later became a nationally known preacher with the Assemblies of God, went for a canoe ride on the Potomac River. We enjoyed the ride so much and got so comfortable in the canoe that we both fell sound asleep.

We drifted toward the falls, and had already been caught in rapids that threatened to hurl us to our deaths, when God spoke to Richard's mother on the campground, told her what was happening, and she began to call on Him to save us by a miracle. Suddenly, Richard and I were both shaken by an invisible power and became wide awake. It was just in time, for only with supernatural help were we able to row away from the dam.

- 108 -

Saved from A Watery Death in the Chesapeake Bay

In 1956, while I pastored in Richmond, Virginia, the president of an insurance company asked me to perform the marriage ceremony for his fiancé and himself. I had been speaking to him about miracles, but he did not believe too much in them.

A couple of weeks after the marriage, the insurance president called me, and said, "Because of your kindness in performing the ceremony, my wife and I want to take you and your family for an outing in our yacht on the Chesapeake Bay." We replied that we would enjoy the trip.

When we got way out in the middle of the bay, we discovered that the yacht was taking on water at an alarming rate. The president immediately got my wife, myself and our three children to bail water with buckets. He became frantic, for, as I remember, we were seven miles out. He said, "The yacht will sink before we get to shore."

I went to praying. I said, "Father, we are candidates for a great miracle. Show this insurance president that God does work miracles today." Then I commanded that God would fill the hole in the bottom of the yacht with a fish or some object. It turned out that there was a hole in the bottom, because someone had cleaned the yacht, and had forgotten to place the stopper back in the bunghole, where they let the water out when they clean the vessel.

When the yacht was put in dry-dock to examine it, they found that some foreign object had been sucked so tightly into the bunghole that the water had stopped coming in, and there was much rejoicing at the miracle of God. The insurance executive told me that it was the greatest miracle that he had ever seen or heard of and, from now on, he would be a firm believer in miracles.

- 109 -

"Doctor, He Does Not Have Heart Trouble"

About 1:30 in the morning, they awakened me as I slept in the church I was building in Texas. They said, "Brother Ward, Brother Tedford wants you to take him to the hospital. He is dying with a heart attack." I was out of gas and the hospital was twenty-one miles away, so we awakened the man who ran the gas station about two miles away, and he sold us a tank of gas.

Out on the highway, Brother Tedford kept crying, "Brother Ward, drive faster. I will die before you get me to the hospital."

I answered, "I am already going 93 miles an hour, and a state trooper just passed me going the opposite direction." I finally got the preacher to the hospital.

In the emergency room, a doctor was giving orders, "This man is dying with a heart attack; do this; do that."

God spoke definitely to me, "He is not having a heart attack; he is having a gall bladder attack." So I went over to the doctor who was screaming out orders and said, "Doctor, this man is not having a heart attack; he is having a gall bladder attack."

The doctor's mouth fell open. He was dumbfounded that a layman would have the audacity to tell a doctor what was wrong with the man.

Since Brother Tedford was in the hands of competent people, I went home. It was the middle of the night, and I had to travel the twenty-one miles back home.

In a couple of days I returned to the hospital to see the preacher. I asked him, "Did they discover that it was your gall bladder and not your heart?"

He answered, "Yes, they found out that it was not my heart, but they had to take my gall bladder out, and now I am feeling fine." Soon he was back home in victory.

But, I will never forget that doctor's face when I told him what was wrong with his patient. I could not help telling him, because I know the voice of God, and when God told me, I felt that I should relay the information to the physician.

- 110 -

"Flying Upside Down, Holding on for Life"

In 1941, I was holding a four-week revival for Brother E.L. Mason in Highlands, Texas. He was a wonderful pilot, and he wanted to take me up in his plane. In that year, people did not have seat belts in their cars, so it never occurred to me that open cockpits in small airplanes had seat belts, and I did not fasten mine.

Brother Mason and I were great friends, and he wanted to give me the thrill of flying in this small plane. He sat in the front cockpit and I sat in the back one. He began doing loops. He was flying upside down. I was screaming at the top of my lungs, holding on by my fingernails. I had my knees tight against the top of the cockpit carriage. The more that I screamed, the more enjoyment he thought that I was having, so he would give me an encore. I did not just scream, I was praying for my life.

When we finally landed, I told Brother Mason that I almost fell out of the plane. Then he did the screaming, "Didn't you have your seat belt fastened?"

I answered, "I didn't even know that there was a seat belt."

His face turned ashen, as it was drained of blood. Then together, we began to thank God for His Divine protection, once again exhibited in my behalf.

- 111 -

A Man Is Brought from Kentucky to Arizona

I was conducting a revival in my big tent in Tucson, Arizona, and some people brought a man on an airplane from Kentucky to be prayed over for healing. He wanted me to pray for him before the church service, and I asked, "Why?"

He answered, "Because I cannot sit down." His body was all twisted like a cork screw. He was only about five feet tall, but I knew that if his body would unwind he would be a tall man.

I told him that I would rather pray for him after church, when I felt that the power of God would be upon me with greater anointing. So he said, "I will go back in the congregation, prop myself up against a quarter pole and stand there as best as I can. All during my sermon, my eyes were drawn to him, leaning his crooked body against the pole.

Toward the end of my sermon, the power of God came mightily upon me. I jumped off the platform, went back to where he was, laid my hand on his head and began praying out loud for him.

Suddenly I heard noises like things cracking and moving in his body. He seemed to be unwinding, and when he stood up straight, he was a tall man. I had never seen anything exactly like this before. With the glory of God upon him, he stood there like an angel. I was overcome. He seemed to be more than a foot taller. I knew that I had seen the power of God in action.

- 112 -

"Come Home Immediately; Bobby Has Polio"

When I was putting up the tent in San Antonio, Texas, getting ready for my first big tent meeting, the folks from home in Tulsa, Oklahoma, called me,

"You must come home immediately, Bobby has polio."

I answered, "This is a real trick of the devil to keep me from starting my tent ministry. I am not coming home, but I will never eat again until God heals my son."

I fasted eighteen days through my first tent meeting. Then I received a call from home, "Bobby has been completely healed."

Today, "Bobby" is the Rev. John Robert Ward, pastor of the Evangel Assemblies of God Church in Richmond, Virginia. He has never had any repercussions from polio. He has absolutely no signs that he ever had the affliction.

- 113 -

The Lepers Are Healed in the Bahamas

In 1950 I was pastor of a church in Tulsa, Oklahoma. I took a month's leave of absence to hold a revival in the Bahama Islands. Evangelist Fern Huffstutler held a revival in my church while I was gone, and some people criticized me, because they said that I was not there when our church enjoyed the greatest revival of its history. But I could never feel bad, for I probably had the greatest revival of my life in the Bahamas.

I was holding a large tent revival in the Bahamas. One night two or three blind people were healed.

The people became so excited that they went all through the Bahama Islands bringing blind people to the meetings. The next night I prayed for two hundred and four blind people, and I can only remember a very few, perhaps four or five who were not healed.

The people became even more excited and were looking for larger fields of opportunity for God to work His miracles. So they asked me to go over to the Leper Colony, and pray for the lepers.

The next day found me at the Leper Colony with Pastor Elvis Davis. They would not allow me to touch the lepers. They had fifty-six lepers come out in the yard, standing almost shoulder to shoulder facing me. The authorities measured off fifty feet from them and drew a line. I could not get closer than fifty feet from the lepers.

I walked down the line and prayed for each leper personally. At the end of the prayer session, I pronounced every leper healed. Then I said, "All those lepers inside the buildings, who were too sick to come out, I pronounce them healed also."

The Bahamian law required a doctor to visit patients every two weeks for a year, before he could pronounce them cured. So Pastor Elvis Davis went with the doctor every two weeks for a solid year. At the end of that time, the doctor declared that all the lepers were cured.

I was in the audience when I heard my great friend, Rev. David Nunn, tell this story, saying that one hundred lepers were healed. I told Brother Nunn that I was the evangelist who prayed for those lepers, but I only remembered fifty-six lepers being healed.

That night I called Pastor Elvis Davis long distance. He was living in Houston, Texas. He informed me that fifty-six lepers had come into the yard for prayer, but reminded me that at the end of my prayers. I had prayed for all the lepers inside the buildings that had not been able to come into the yard and had pronounced them healed also. He stated, "There were, all together, one hundred lepers, counting those who were inside and outside."

They were all pronounced cured by the doctor after spending a full year inspecting each one of them.

God put the leper colony in the Bahama Islands out of business, for they closed the leper colony up after all the patients were released, and the colony has remained shut until this day. I personally know of at least two of the lepers, who were healed and released, who became Assemblies of God ministers, for they called me long distance, telling me that they had been healed and had become ministers.

- 114 -

"I Broke That Wild Horse"

When I was conducting a revival meeting in Bartlesville, Oklahoma, in 1942, I was asked to go by and pray for a man on my way to church one night.

The sick man told me, "I have been to Mayo Clinic in Minnesota twice, and to two other nationally known clinics, but they could not help me. I have a tumor on the pituitary gland, and I cannot lie on a flat surface or I will go unconscious. I cannot sit up or I will go unconscious, and I cannot stand up or I will go unconscious. I have to lie on an inclined plane with my head higher than my feet."

I prayed for him and then said, "While you have been lying here, you have been looking out of the window, day after day, and there is something that you have been wanting to do for a long time. I have to go to church now, but I believe that God has healed you. So whatever it is that you have wanted to do, when I leave, get up and in the Name of Jesus, go out and do it."

That night, when I was sitting on the platform, getting ready to preach, I saw the man and his wife come in the front door of the church. They walked up to me, and he said, "Preacher, don't preach yet. I want to tell you something. After you prayed for me, I knew that I was healed. Then I looked out of the window and saw the wild horse that we have out back. I used to be a cowboy and for a long time, I have been looking out that back window at the wild horse and wishing I could break him. You told me to do what I had been wanting to do. So do you know what I did before church tonight? I went out there and broke that wild horse. I am totally healed! Hallelujah!"

- 115 -

The River That Makes Glad

During the Great Depression I was pastor in Attleboro, Massachusetts. I was only twenty years old and was $600 in debt. I was supporting five people on ten or fifteen dollars a week. I saw no way that I could pay my debt, but God gave me a revelation when I read in His Word: *"There is a river, the streams whereof shall make glad the city of God, the holy place of the tabernacles of the most High"* (Psalm 46:4).

About nine o'clock one morning, I sat on a chair in our kitchen, and all day long I said, "There is a RIVER, there IS a river, there is a river THAT SHALL MAKE GLAD." I don't think that I said any other words than these all day long. I sat there until probably three in the afternoon. Then I jumped into the river that by faith I could see flowing right through my kitchen. Then, as my faith increased, I took every one of my debts and threw them in the river. I said, "I drown my debts in the river that makes glad."

Soon there was a knock on the door. Three people came in: a deacon, Ad Powers, his mother, and a lady in the church. They said, "We understand that you have a debt of $93.00. Please give us the papers on that, and we are going to pay $31.00 a piece and pay that debt for you.

I gave them the papers. When they left, I began to

shout, "Dear God I see how THIS RIVER MAKES GLAD."

As I was shouting, there was another knock on the door. Someone came in and said, "God tells me that you have a debt of so much money. Just give me the papers. I want to pay that debt for you." I gave him the papers on the debt.

When he left, it was not long until someone else knocked on the door, saying, "I could not sleep all last night. God told me that you have a debt of so much money, and He told me to pay it for you. Just give me the papers. I will gladly pay it right away."

I tell you that I slept in victory that night. I had thrown the $600 of debt into THE RIVER THAT MAKES GLAD, and I was full of joy; for God saw to it, even in the middle of the Great Depression, that the entire amount was paid quickly, and I did not have to pay a penny of it myself. I learned a lesson that has helped me through the years. When I get a burden too hard to carry, I head for THE RIVER THAT MAKES GLAD and hurl my burdens and problems into God's River

- 116 -

My Tonsils Were Not Cut, Burned or Pulled Out

In 1937, when I was twenty-one years old, I went to see a Jewish doctor in Providence, Rhode Island. I said, "Doctor, please examine my tonsils." He looked at my tonsils and enumerated seven diseases that I would contract if I did not have my tonsils removed.

I went home and prayed for myself, and if you will pardon my saying it, I had to spit up a bunch of cohesive matter, pus and blood. I knelt down and continued to pray. I then had to arise and spit up more of the same matter.

The next day I returned to see the same Jewish doctor and declared, "Doctor, I want you to examine my tonsils."

He answered, "What is the matter with you? I just examined them yesterday."

"Well," I replied, "will you not examine them again today, please?"

He put a stick on my tongue, nearly choked me, and said, "Say 'Ah.' " He dropped the stick on the floor, crying, "What has happened to you?"

I answered, "You tell me."

He declared, "Your tonsils are as perfect as a new born baby's"

I stated, "I have been to see my Doctor."

He declared, "Listen, there is no doctor in the world that can extract the poison out of tonsils. They either cut the tonsils out, burn them out, or pull them out, but they cannot take the poison matter out and leave the tonsils there."

I answered, "My Doctor just removes the poison."

He shouted, "Who is your doctor?"

I replied, "The Lord Jesus Christ, my Savior and your Messiah."

He gave a little scream, grabbed his hat, ran out of the office, down the corridor, and down the steps. I looked out of the window and saw him come out of the ground floor entrance. I watched him run down the street until he was out of sight.

There were eight or ten people waiting in his outer office to see him, and I waited about a half hour to see if I owed him any money, but he did not come back. He saw a miracle that day, and he was running to tell somebody about it.

- 117 -

Staying in the Home of Rev. R.L. Scarbrough

In Cincinnati, I stayed in the home of the Rev. and Mrs. R.L. Scarbrough. One day he told me, "I have just written a book, and I am going to the bank and borrow $1,328.00 to pay for the publishing of it." That was Friday.

I told him, "Do not borrow the money from the bank. Tuesday, you will receive $1,328.00 in the mail."

On Tuesday he received two letters in the mail. Each one had money in it. One had over $800 in it and one had over $500 in it. Together the two letters contained exactly $1,328.00.

God knows what we have need of, and He will supply according to His riches in Glory.

- 118 -

Miracles with Children

God has given me great success in praying for the healing of children. I remember so clearly praying for a four-year-old boy in Caracas, Venezuela. He could not walk, but when he began walking and running around the church, many people of the church began running with him, so that they could watch the excitement on his face.

One time before church in Carlsbad, New Mexico, a father asked me to watch his boy run down the aisle of the church and back to the front, where I was sitting. The father said, "You don't understand why I asked my boy to run in church, do you?"

I answered, "I have no idea why."

He continued, "Because my boy could not walk and you prayed for him, and now he can walk and run beautifully. I wanted you to see it several years after you prayed for him."

- 119 -

A Lady Is Healed of Polio

I was preaching in a large tent in Plainview, Texas, and right in the middle of my sermon a lady stood up and began to walk and run, making quite a bit of noise. I said, "Sister, I am trying to preach. Please be quiet."

A lady who was with her spoke for her, saying, "This sister had polio when she was young. One leg was much narrower and shorter than the other. All her life she has limped seriously. And just now, while you were preaching, God sent His Word and healed her. For the first time in her life, both legs are the same size, and she is able to walk and run normally. That is why she is making so much noise."

I answered, "Make all the noise that you want to, sister. Run again. Help yourself. God is so good."

- 120 -

Deafness Was Healed Instantly

For five or six years, God gave me phenomenal success in praying for deaf people. During that time, as far as I know, I never prayed for a deaf person that was not healed, and many hundreds of deaf folks were instantly healed. But then, because it seemed so easy to heal the deaf, I began to ask God to give me power, under Him, over much harder cases.

I may have been out of order in my talk to God. I don't know. But from that day until now, and it is probably fifteen to eighteen years that have gone by, I have very seldom seen God heal a deaf person in my meetings.

- 121 -

Oral Roberts' Tent Was Given to Rex Humbard

One day when I was praying for a new tent, Oral Roberts said to me, "I am giving you my new tent. I paid $40,000 for it, and I have only used it one time. It seats ten thousand people, and I want you to have it. You come over Thursday a week, and I will have it ready for you."

But a day or two before I was to pick it up, Oral said to me, "Rex Humbard's tent blew down last night. He had Sister Katherine Kuhlman of Pittsburgh holding him a revival. They had ten thousand people coming to the revival every night. Now, they don't know what to do. They have no place to go to continue the meetings. Brother Humbard called me last night. He really needs help. Now, I know that I gave you that new tent of mine, and I am not an Indian giver, so I leave it entirely up to you."

I answered, "Brother Roberts, give that tent to Rex Humbard. He needs it now." So Oral Roberts gave the tent to Brother Humbard. For legal purposes, he sold it to him for one dollar. I don't even know if Rex Humbard ever knew that I was also involved in his getting the tent or not. He put the tent up immediately, continuing the revival without much of a break.

Many hundreds of people were saved and other hundreds of people were healed in the meetings. I know that Oral Roberts will get a big reward in

Heaven for what he did, as Rex Humbard built his great temple, seating five thousand, in Akron, Ohio, and the tent made a large contribution to it. I also hope that the Lord will remember that I had a small part in it, too.

- 122 -

I Was Baptized in the Holy Spirit

The day before I was baptized in the Holy Spirit, I was baptized in water in the Potomac River in West Virginia. I was so thrilled and filled with God that I got lost in the Spirit, and after I was baptized in water I began to float downstream. I did not fully realize what was going on. I was so happy, but when I opened my eyes, I was probably a good fifty feet downstream from the other people who were being baptized in water. When I came out of the water, I was so full of the Holy Spirit that I laid right on the bank and praised God long after everyone else had left the scene.

The day before, I was so desirous of the baptism of the Holy Ghost that I had told the Lord that I would never eat another bite of food or drink another drop of water until He baptized me in the Holy Ghost. I had told Him, "I would rather die than live without the baptism of the Holy Spirit. So if you do not want me to have the baptism of the Spirit, you might as well make room for me in Heaven."

The next night after I was baptized in water, Sunday night, I had gone three days without eating. That seemed like a long time to a sixteen-year-old boy. I had a headache, and during the altar service after church, I said, "Dear Lord, I am too sick to get the baptism of the Holy Spirit tonight. Every other night I have praised God louder and longer than anyone else, I have clapped my hands harder than others, and I still did not get the baptism of the Spirit. So I know that I cannot get the baptism tonight, for I am too sick to go through that performance. I have a headache, and I am going to my tent and go to sleep. But before I go to bed, Lord, I am going to kneel at the altar and say good night to Jesus."

It was the third Sunday in August in 1932. At the altar, I got on my knees and said, "Good night, Jesus." Immediately, I saw a great ball of fire coming down out of Heaven, getting closer and closer. It came through the ceiling of that tabernacle at the Falling Waters Campmeeting of the Assemblies of God in West Virginia. I watched that ball of fire hit me in the chest. When it hit me, I fell over in the sawdust and began to speak in a heavenly language that I had never learned. I was speaking in an unknown tongue just like the one hundred and twenty people in the upper room, mentioned in the Bible in Acts 2:4.

They told me later that a drunken man had come off the highway onto the campground, heard me speaking in the heavenly language, and drew his foot back to kick me. His foot was paralyzed in that position. The last that anyone ever heard of him, he had hopped off the campground and still could not bend his leg. I never knew anything about it, except what I was told, but I am persuaded that when we are filled with His Spirit, God protects us from harm and danger.

When I arose from the sawdust at 12:30 in the morning, I was so happy and so thrilled in having the baptism of the Holy Spirit. I had a bomb of love burst in my soul. I hugged every boy and man that was around in the tabernacle at that hour. I hugged every tree that got in my way between the tabernacle and my tent. When I got in the tent, I hugged the tent pole. Then I lay on my bed and talked in that heavenly language all night. Nobody had to tell me that I had received the baptism of the Holy Spirit. I knew what had happened to me. And, as I look back on that moment, after sixty-two years, I know unequivocally that it was the experience that changed my life.

Thirteen years after I received the baptism of the Holy Spirit, I was asked to be a professor in one of the best Christian colleges in America, but it was specified that I would have to give up my belief in the baptism of the Holy Spirit with the initial evidence of speaking in other tongues. They told me, "If you give up this idea, we will make you head of the Department of Philosophy in the college."

I answered, "If there is anything in the world that I am absolutely certain about beyond the scintilla of a doubt, it is that I have the baptism of the Holy Ghost, and I have spoken in other tongues. I don't know when I got saved, for I was born into this thing, and I got 'saved' under every evangelist that came to our church in Washington, D.C., when I was a boy. I got 'saved' under Otto J. Klink, I got 'saved' under Watson Argue, I got 'saved' under Edith Mae Pennington. I guess I got 'saved' hundreds of times. I don't know which inoculation 'took.' I know that I am saved, but I can't tell you when it happened.

However, I know exactly when I received the baptism of the Holy Ghost. I know the year and the month. I know the week and the day. I know the hour. I know the place. I know when I received the baptism of the Holy Spirit, and I know that it is real. How then could you expect me to deny this, the most wonderful experience that ever came into my life?"

After I received the baptism of the Holy Ghost, God led me out into preaching immediately. Two weeks after that wonderful experience, the greatest young preacher that I knew in America, Rev. J. Robert Ashcroft, asked me to go to North Carolina with him to help in his revival. As doors opened to me to preach, it even surprised me.

- 123 -

My Mother Saw the King and Queen of England

There are different kinds of miracles. There are miracles of finance, miracles of healings, and then there are miracles of love, where God just loves to delight our hearts. It was one of these miracles of delight that I would like to discuss with you now.

When the King and Queen of England visited Washington, D.C., I believe that it was in 1941, I was telling my mother that I had been privileged to see them on three different occasions. She said, "Oh, I would have loved to have seen them."

So right in our living room I prayed with my mother. I said, "Oh, Lord, You know that the King and Queen of England are scheduled to return to England tomorrow. Please let my mother see the King and Queen before they return to their homeland."

I felt led to hurry my mother. We were going downtown. I said, "Hurry Mama."

We got in the car and began driving toward town. We only lived one block from a main boulevard. We were on a lonely stretch of pavement, and we had not gone more than four or five blocks from our house, when I looked in the rearview mirror and saw a chauffeur driving President and Mrs. Franklin D. Roosevelt and the King and Queen of England in an open car right behind us.

I hurried, got ahead of them, and stopped our car at the side of the road. My mother and I got out and stood beside our car at the side of the road. We were the only ones there. We waved at the President and Mrs. Roosevelt and at the King and Queen of England. Their car slowed up and almost stopped in front of us, and all four of them waved at us and spoke a cheery remark. They could not have been more than eight to ten feet from us. It made us so very happy. My mother said, "It did not take long for that prayer to be answered."

Moreover, I must tell you that it will not take much time for your serious prayers to be answered either, for the Lord desires to grant your requests. He loves to have happy children.

- 124 -

Singing in Front of the White House

One day when I was sixteen years old and was walking in front of the White House in Washington, D.C., I told God, "The man who is in that house, the President of the United States, must have had a call on his life to be chosen to be President of this great nation."

God spoke to me, "You have a call on your life. I have called you to represent Me, and I want you to go at this time and pastor the Sand Flat church, out in the country."

I answered, "Oh, Lord, I cannot go there. I am a city boy, and that is two hundred and fifty miles from home, and way out in the country. I don't even know where I would stay. It would be too lonesome. I could not take it. But, Dear Lord, if you will come down, take my hand, and walk with me, and talk with me, I will go."

Instantly I felt a presence next to me, and I felt a hand take hold of my hand. My hand began to jump as though a thousand needles with electric vibrations had gone through it. Then my hand became suddenly still, and I had the sense that it was in the grip of another hand.

As I walked along in front of the White House, I began singing at the top of my voice. People that passed me on the street must have thought that I was crazy, but I was singing lustily, "I'll go where You want me to go, Dear Lord, I'll be what You want me to be. I'll do what You want me to do."

I am sure that the President of the United States inside the White House could not have felt more chosen and more needed than I felt as I walked outside the White House, feeling that I was definitely chosen of God.

I pastored the Sand Flat church in the country in the state of Maryland for one year, and when I left, I got them to accept my sister and brother-in-law as pastors. They also stayed a year and were able to come directly to Richmond, Virginia, when they left there. They started a great work in Richmond that is still going strong after sixty and more years.

I am sure that God has definitely chosen you, also, for some important work that He wants you to do.

- 125 -

Put Twenty Dollars Worth of Gas in the Car

In Fremont, Ohio, I was conducting a revival. I pulled into a gas station to get gas. I had ten dollars, but I said, "Dear Lord, I wish that I could get twenty dollars worth of gas, but I only have ten dollars."

Just then a lady drove alongside of my car and said, "I saw you pull into this gas station, so I turned around and came back. God told me to buy your gas for you. So use this twenty dollars to buy gas."

When you walk and talk with God, He is mindful of every need that you have and takes care of it, and He is always on time.

- 126 -

My Son Billy Swallowed a Pendant

One day, when our son, William A. Ward, III, was only a baby, my wife came home saying, "I am sure that Billy swallowed the pendant that I had on a chain around my neck."

I answered, "Oh, you are just imagining that. He wouldn't do that."

She said, "I am not just imagining it. I was in the grocery store, and he was in my arms, playing with the pendant. Suddenly I missed the pendant. We could not find it on the floor or anywhere. I am sure that Billy had to swallow it."

I replied, "Well, we will go get an x-ray and make sure." We had the x-ray made, and sure enough, there was the pendant inside the baby, and it looked so big.

The doctor said, "We will have to operate on him and get it out."

I replied, "Doctor, we are going to pray, and the Lord will let him pass it."

The doctor looked relieved and answered, "Well, it is perfectly smooth, and it can't hurt him. You watch his stool, and we will wait a couple of days." We watched his stool, and sure enough, the pendant came out easily and never caused the baby any pain.

It is so wonderful to be a Christian; God takes care of every phase of your life.

- 127 -

She Is Brain-dead and Does Not Know Anything

A man, Al Perry, whom I had played handball with at the YMCA for probably more than thirty years, asked me to go to the hospital and pray for his wife. He said, "She is brain-dead, and the doctors and the family have decided to turn the life-support system off. But before we do, we would like you to pray for her, to make sure that she goes to Heaven."

I asked her husband to hold off, not turn the life

supports off, but to give me a little time with her. I made five or six trips to the hospital and prayed for her quite a few times. Each time she got better. I would say, "We are going to give our heart to Christ. If you want to do this, squeeze my hand." She squeezed my hand tightly. Often I asked her, "Do you love Jesus? If you do, squeeze my hand." She always squeezed my hand. I would say to her, "You are going to Heaven to be with Jesus. Do you love Him? Do you know what I am saying to you? If you do, squeeze my hand." She would squeeze my hand tightly.

Then the husband told me that the doctors and family had decided that I had enough time with her, and they were going to turn the life-support systems off. My friend asked me to preach her funeral, because I had been with her so much in the hospital. I was able to tell people at the funeral service that I knew that she had given her heart to Christ, even though they said her brain was dead, and that I knew that she loved Jesus and was ready for Heaven.

The husband told me, "You comforted the family, and we will never forget you."

- 128 -

The Church Building in Richmond Is Bought

In 1955, I came to Richmond to see my sister and brother-in-law. My brother-in-law said, "There is a church building that I would like to buy."

I asked, "Why don't you buy it?"

He answered, "I don't have the money."

I replied, "I don't have the money either, but I could buy that church building." The next day, I said, "Let's go by and see that church building."

It was a large, beautiful brick church building on the corner, on a main street. I was told that it was the biggest church building in Richmond under one roof. It had eighty-five rooms in it, seven auditoriums and seven restrooms.

My brother-in-law and I sat in the car looking at the building for a while. I said, "Go in and buy that building." He maintained that he could not afford it. I said, "Well, all that I have is ten dollars, but if you don't buy it, I will."

He replied, "I want to see you do it." He waited in the car, and I went in and bought the building. I said, "I will put ten dollars down on the contract to seal the sale. I will pay you one hundred and fifty dollars a month rent until the purchase price of fifty thousand dollars is paid in full. You can still use the church building every Sunday morning, and we will only use it Sunday afternoons and every night in the week."

Because I had bought the building, I was obligated to stay there. We had service every night for five years. I stayed there a total of eleven years. Then Brother and Sister Heflin came over and bought the building, and they have been there now twenty-eight years. They are on three radio stations every Sunday, and have been on two of the stations for almost the entire time that they have been in the building.

After they had bought the building, Brother Heflin, Sr. stood in the aisle of the church, took my hand, and said, "God bless this man." Then he prophesied, "As long as you live, you will always have a place to preach in this church." So as long as they have had the building, the Heflins have had me preach five or ten minutes before the regular sermon every Sunday morning that I am in town.

Now the Heflins have not only the large church building in Richmond, but what I consider to be one of the greatest campmeetings in the world just fifteen miles away in Ashland, Virginia. And both the church and campmeeting are still growing rapidly.

- 129 -

The Orson Welles Radio Program Hoax

As a young boy, five to ten years old, I was stirred by the tremendous revivals of Aimee Semple McPherson, Rev. Smith Wigglesworth, and F.F. Bosworth. All three of these great meetings were healing campaigns where the ministers prayed for the sick, and I thoroughly believed in them, for not only were the ministers praying for the souls of people, they were also praying for their bodies, too. Even at my young age, I felt that the Gospel of Jesus Christ should be all-embracing, all-inclusive, as to bless not only the souls of people, but also to take care of their physical needs through the vicissitudes of life.

So, when I, as a seventeen-year-old boy, was preaching in the coal mining regions of West Virginia, Pennsylvania, and Maryland, I preached a saving, healing Christ. One night I was preaching a revival in a little schoolhouse in Lonaconing, Maryland. As I was preaching on the subject of Hell, the furnace in the basement broke, and smoke began to pour up through the floor. The smoke filled the room until it was difficult for me to see the people. It was such a realistic scene that every sinner in the house came to the altar for salvation.

A few weeks later, I was conducting a revival in Kitzmiller, Maryland, and I was preaching again on the subject of Hell. As I gave the altar call, conviction lay heavily upon the congregation. Suddenly a lady came screaming in the front door of the church. She cried, "Folks, forgive me for disturbing the service, but I just listened to Orson Welles' radio program, and he said that men from Mars have invaded New York City, and they are coming this way. People are fleeing this way by the thousands, trying to escape these men from Mars. The men from Mars will be here in a few minutes."

The woman was so hysterical that fear gripped that audience. People began to scream and dropped down on their knees, praying as loud as they could. Every sinner in the house seemed to be converted that night, but I imagine that they all backslid the next day when they found out that the radio program had been a great hoax, and that men from Mars had not invaded New York City. I have often wondered if people would carry on like that, screaming and shouting, when it was not real, what are they going to do when it is real, and judgment does fall upon the Earth?

- 130 -

My Mother Really Was Dying

While I was in Windsor, North Carolina, helping J. Robert Ashcroft in his revival, I felt that my mother was dying. In those days we did not have the great network of telephones, so I could not call home. I was completely isolated, staying at a farmhouse with church people.

I was completely overwhelmed with this feeling that my mother was dying, but I thought that it was my first experience of real homesickness, for it was my first time away from home for any extended period. I was under such a burden of intercessory prayer for my mother that I would get deathly ill myself and would have to go vomit.

As I prayed for my mother, in a vision I could see our house and crepe on the front door, signifying that there was death in the house. I prayed until I felt that God had heard me and healed my mother. When I returned home, I found my mother well. So I never told her of my prayer for her healing, as I was convinced that I must have been terribly homesick.

But just before my mother died, twenty years later,

my mother said, "William, do you remember the time that you were in Windsor, North Carolina, with Brother Ashcroft?"

I answered, "Yes."

Mother continued, "I have never told you this, but I almost died when you were down there. I was seized with a heart attack and was unconscious for several hours. I was sick in bed for several days, and they gave up hope for me and thought that I was dying. I felt that I was dying, also."

I answered, "Mama, I didn't know that. All these twenty years I have thought that I must have been terribly homesick as it was my first experience away from home for such an extended period. But while I was there I fasted and prayed for your healing, because I felt that surely you were dying, and I had a terrible burden of prayer placed upon me to pray through for your recovery."

- 131 -

Six Hundred Dollars Blew Out of His Pocket

A man in Texas came to me asking me to pray for him to get a better job. I said, "If you will pay your tithes, God will give you a better job." In a day or two he had a new job, paying him over $600 dollars a week, which was very good wages in those days.

But he came to me, when he received his first paycheck of over $600, and he was very sad. He said, "I was coming down a country road on my motorcycle. I was going fast, and my pay check flew out of my shirt pocket. It blew over the fence and out into a field, where the grass was in places waist high. I hunted for it for an hour or two, but I could not find it. I doubt if I can ever find it."

I reiterated, "If you will pay your tithes, God will let you find that check easily." I prayed for him. He went back to the field, and in five or ten minutes he found that pay check.

God is in this thing with us. He will always do His part if we will do our part.

- 132 -

A Man from India Finds Me in Virginia

In 1993 a man came from India, determined to find me, and ask me to come to India to preach. He arrived at my sister's and nephew's campmeeting in Ashland, Virginia, the week that I was preaching every night. Someone in India had given him one of my old magazines with my picture in it and stated that I was conducting a revival meeting in the First Assembly of God Church in Kansas City, Missouri. He did not know that my picture in the magazine was about forty years old.

So he began asking different people how to get to Kansas City, Missouri. He told someone that he was going to Kansas City to get William A. Ward to go to

India. He was told, "You do not have to go to Kansas City to find that man; he is the one who is preaching every night at this camp." He was astonished because he was looking for a much younger man. Nevertheless he was happy to find me and invite me to India, where he had several hundred churches.

I call this a miracle, because God saved the Indian preacher from making a fruitless trip of approximately three thousand miles (round trip), and let him know that the preacher he came to America to find was the evangelist that he was listening to each night.

- 133 -

A House Trailer Is Unhurt in Rocky Mount, North Carolina

The late Dr. Wallace Heflin, Jr., my nephew, and I were conducting a revival in the high school auditorium in Rocky Mount, North Carolina. We were staying in the home of Brother and Sister Baines. Sister Baines is a well-known preacher who has ministered much overseas. Sunday, I was on my way to the afternoon meeting. Brother Heflin had already left for the service. I had just gone out the front door and was going down the steps, when Brother Baines came to the door and said, "Brother Ward, will you pray that God will protect our house trailer? The television says that a terrible tornado is coming right through here."

I stood on the steps and prayed God to protect the trailer home and everything in it. Then I went to the service.

At the close of the service, a man announced to the crowd, "Let us pray for Brother and Sister Baines, as their home has been destroyed by the tornado."

I could not believe what I was hearing. I said, "Dear Lord, I don't believe a word of that. I stood on the front steps and prayed that You would completely protect that home, and I know that You heard my prayer." All the way that I drove home, I kept talking to God, and saying, "It is impossible that the trailer is destroyed, because I prayed, and You answer prayer."

When I reached the home, I saw the brick house directly across the street was in very bad shape. Furniture had been sucked out the front window, leaving a large, gaping hole in the bricks. Every brick house around the trailer had been badly damaged. I saw that a large tree in front of the trailer had been uprooted and was leaning over the trailer, but not touching it.

When I knocked on the door, Brother Baines opened it, saying, "Come in and see the miracle. Not one thing on or in our house has been hurt. Even all these knickknacks on the shelves have not been turned over."

He said, "I was lying on the sofa in the living room, looking out the window, and I saw the large tree in the front uprooted. It began to fall toward the house, but suddenly it stopped coming toward me and just hung in the air. If it had hit, it would probably have killed me, as it was falling toward me."

I just threw my hands up and thanked God that I had not believed the erroneous report given at the service. In my heart I had known that God heard our prayer. He is a protector and a deliverer, and He is *"A very present help in time of trouble"* (Psalm 46:1).

- 134 -

I Could Not Leave the City

I closed my open air revival in Breckenridge, Texas, said good-bye to all the folks, got in my car and started to drive away. But the Lord would not let me leave. I drove around the block a couple of times, and then came back, because God told me, "Do not leave yet; a man has come to see you."

I stopped at the revival site. A man said, "Oh, I am so glad that you came back. We have been traveling many miles, and we were late. We just drove up. I am totally deaf, and I have come to be healed."

We placed our hands on his ears, prayed a simple prayer, and God instantly healed him, so that he could easily hear a watch tick in both ears.

I must reiterate that I am no healer. If any man would tell me that he was a healer, I would have no confidence in him. I would shun him as I would a plague. If anyone is healed in our meetings, it is God who does it, so to God be the glory.

After the man was healed, then I felt a perfect release to leave town, and I started on the road to my next revival.

- 135 -

A Blind Man Was Healed After We Left the Room

In 1935, in Providence, Rhode Island, another preacher and I went to pray for a blind man. The preacher asked me to pray for the man. I answered, "Before I pray, I feel that I should read the eleventh chapter of Hebrews." I read this wonderful faith chapter: *"By faith, Abraham ... By faith, Isaac ... By faith, Jacob ... By faith, Joseph ... By faith, ... By faith, ..."* Then I prayed, but nothing happened. The man was not healed.

The preacher and I went back out in the cold, going back to the church. The preacher said, "Brother Ward, I am ashamed of you. It is your fault that the blind man was not healed. You read that entire chapter of Hebrews, and you got that man so worn out that he did not have faith for his healing."

Well, I felt smaller and smaller. I thought, "I feel so small; he will not have to open the door to the church for me; I will just slide under the door."

Suddenly we heard a big noise behind us. We turned and there came the blind man running and shouting. He exclaimed, "I have been running after you for five blocks, shouting, trying to attract your attention. After you left, I was healed."

The other preacher began testing his eyesight: "What color necktie do I have on?" "Describe my clothes." "What is that man doing?" The fellow described everything perfectly.

The preacher asked him, "How is it that you were healed after we left, and you were not healed while we were there?"

The man answered, "After you left, I began quoting the eleventh chapter of Hebrews: *'By faith, Abraham ... By faith, Moses ... By faith, Rahab ... By faith, Samson ...,'* and then," he said, "I cried, 'By faith I see,' and the scales fell off my eyes, and I could see. I have been running down the street, trying to catch you and tell you that I am healed."

I was just a young seventeen-year-old preacher and, needless to say, I felt better that I would no longer have to berate myself that I had caused the man not to be healed. Actually God showed me that I had listened to Him and read the eleventh chapter of Hebrews, because He used that scripture to raise the man's faith to the victory level.

- 136 -

Please Pray Your Very Best Prayer

In 1937, I was preaching a revival in Belvoir, Virginia. One night the preacher said to me, "Brother

Ward, I want you to pray your very best prayer for a man who has come to church. He has two cancers in his face, and the cancers have made an awful hole in his face."

The man knelt at the altar for prayer. I went over and placed my hand on his head. I did not pray out loud, just left my hand on his head for a minute or so, then went back to my seat on the platform.

Nothing seemed to happen. The man was not healed.

I was staying in the pastor's house, and when we went home after church, he said to me, "Brother Ward, I am ashamed of you. I asked you to pray your very best prayer, and you didn't even open your mouth."

Well, I got my Bible out and read out loud, *"They shall lay hands on the sick* [and pray their very best prayer] *and they shall recover."* I continued to read, *"They shall lay hands on the sick* [and prophesy, and if the people like the prophecy], *they shall recover."* I made it worse, *"They shall lay hands on the sick* [and jump three feet high and turn a somersault], *and they shall recover."*

"Is that what the Bible says, preacher? No, it simply reads, *'They shall lay hands on the sick, and they shall recover'*" (Mark 16:18).

I said, "I did my part in laying my hands on the man's head, and if he is healed, God will have to do His part. He is the Healer. I am no healer. I could not heal anyone."

I was holding a revival in Washington, D.C., several years later. I had rented the Masonic Temple. It was so packed with people standing around the wall, that the firemen made two hundred and eighty-six people leave the building, because of the fire code.

After church a man came to me, asking, "Do you remember praying for a man in Belvoir, Virginia, who had two large cancers on his face?"

I answered, "Yes, Sir, that incident was indelibly stamped on the pages of my memory. I can never forget that."

He declared, "Well, I am that man. When I went home that night, I was washing my face in the sink, and the two cancers fell out. I preserved them in a jar of alcohol, and I have them in the car. I will go out and bring them in now, so that you can see what God did when you prayed."

He soon came back with two large, ugly cancers in the jar of alcohol. I asked him, "What about the big hole that you had in your face?"

He answered, "God gave me a new face."

- 137 -

It Is No Use to Pray for That Man

I was conducting an open air revival in Cambridge, Maryland. They brought an eighty-year-old man up for prayer. He was totally deaf. I started to pray for the fellow, and the pastor said, "There is no use to pray for that man. He is more than seventy years old, and God does not heal people after they are seventy years old, because they have already lived their allotted space of time. He is living on borrowed time."

I responded, "I don't think that God stops loving people because they are over seventy years of age. I think that God loves people after they are seventy, just as much as He does before they are seventy."

I was only twenty-three years old then, and I am glad that I believed that way, because as I write this, I am now over eighty years old myself. I know that I was right in my belief then, because I am conscious that God loves me very much.

At any rate, I went ahead and prayed for the old gentleman, and he did not seem to be healed. But the next night, in the middle of my sermon, this fellow jumped up on the bench, where he had been seated. He began to shout at the top of his voice, "I can hear! I can hear! I am healed! I can hear his sermon! I can hear every word that the preacher is saying! I am healed! I can hear!"

Well, there was no need for me to try and finish my sermon that night. The entire congregation arose as one person and came to the altar for praise and thanksgiving. I believe that the preacher discovered that God does heal people after they are over seventy years old. Hallelujah!

- 138 -

A World Evangelist Was Called in Ice Cream Parlor

I went into an ice cream parlor in Sanford, North Carolina, with Rev. and Mrs. Lloyd Ashby. A lady came to our table to wait on us. I asked if I could take her hand. She wondered what was going on. I prophesied, "God has called you to preach, and you will preach all over the world."

She went back into the kitchen and told people there, "See that man over there? He is crazy. He just told me that I am going to preach all over the world. I am no preacher. I am manager of this ice cream parlor, and I have been here for sixteen years. I have not been traveling anywhere."

A few short years later Jane Lowder began to travel the nations of the world preaching. At the time of this writing, she has traveled in more than sixty-five nations preaching the Gospel. She has been used of God in other nations to bring the message of the baptism of the Holy Spirit to Presbyterian seminaries and other denominational Bible colleges.

This summer Jane Lowder was the only local girl asked to preach at the Calvary Pentecostal summer campmeeting, and she had the largest crowds of any evangelist during the summer.

Today, as I write about Jane Lowder, my local newspaper, *The Richmond Times Dispatch*, has come out with a two-page spread about her preaching. It contains four pictures. Of all the people who travel the world for God, she stands out as one of the greatest souls that I have seen God use for His glory.

I often think how God reached down in an ice cream parlor one night, when the place was filled with young people, who came in for refreshments after a local high school football game. Three preachers were squeezed into a corner of the place. It did not give God much room to work, but He did work, and many nations have been touched because of it.

- 139 -

Healings in Longview, Washington

Some of the healings that were recorded in the Ward tent revival in Longview, Washington, include a sixteen-year-old boy who was born with a paralyzed bladder. No doctor could correct his trouble. He had not been able to attend school or join in the activities of children his age. He was instantly healed and could live a normal life.

A man who was deaf and who suffered with arthritis in his spine and hands was instantly healed.

A man who had a blood clot in his left leg and a terrible case of arthritis was totally healed.

Lewis Agee had a deformed back, which made him very humpbacked for twenty-five years. He was instantly healed and stood up six to eight inches taller after prayer.

- 140 -

I Dreamed of My Niece's Death

I had a dream in 1964 that I went into Bliley's Funeral Parlor in Richmond, and I saw my sister's name on the board, as the one who had died, but when I looked in the casket, it was not my sister but a member of her family (a part of her). I heard a voice say that she died on the second day of campmeeting.

I told the dream to my sister. I said, "I dreamed that someone in your family (someone who was part of you) died on the second day of campmeeting."

On the second night of the campmeeting that year, my sister's oldest child, Mary Elizabeth Henderson (we called her Betty) left the campmeeting and went to bed with a migraine headache. She died in her sleep.

God had used the dream I had to assure my sister and her family that everything was all right. Brother Heflin, Sr. asked me to preach the funeral.

When I walked into the funeral home, I saw that they had my sister's name on the board as the one who had died, just as I had dreamed it. I told them that they had the wrong name on the board, but they would not change it. When other members of the family came in and told them that they had the wrong name on the board, they still would not change it.

Finally, my sister had to go to the officials of the funeral home and assure them that she was Edith W. Heflin, and that she was not dead, before they would change the name on the board to Mary Elizabeth Henderson, the correct name.

Betty was the same girl who, when she was six years old, had cried to go with me from Massachusetts to Virginia to see her mother and father. God told me not to take her, and I had put a trunk where she would have sat.

On the way we suffered an accident. The car turned over, and the trunk was thrown more than fifty feet over a fence into a field, and was destroyed. God saved Betty's life that day. At the time of her death, she was married and had four children. These children are helpers at the great Heflin campmeeting today.

- 141 -

My Aunt Lost Her Voice for Twenty-five Years

My mother was one of the first people in America to receive the baptism of the Holy Ghost with the initial evidence of speaking in other tongues. She went to Azusa Street in Los Angeles, but did not receive the Holy Spirit until she returned to Ohio in 1908.

Her family did not approve of her having this new experience of speaking in tongues. They caused her quite a bit of heartache. I cannot say for sure that it was this oppression which caused my aunt to lose her voice, but it certainly might have been.

Aunt Rebecca was scolding her sister, my mother, for having this experience, when suddenly she lost her voice, and could not speak above a whisper for twenty-five years. They lived in Birmingham, Alabama.

One day when my mother and I were visiting with her relatives in Birmingham, my mother asked me to pray God to heal Aunt Rebecca and give her voice back to her. I may have been around nineteen years old. I laid my hand on the neck of Aunt Rebecca and prayed the prayer of faith. Immediately her voice returned to her, loud and clear. After twenty-five years of silence, her voice was completely normal again. It was a beautiful miracle.

- 142 -

An Eighty-Mile-an-Hour Wind Quieted

In my revival in Albuquerque, New Mexico, I had just begun to preach when an eighty-mile-an-hour wind hit the tent. There were, at the very least, about five thousand people in the tent. At that time we had seven center tent poles made of wood. They were thirty five feet tall and weighed approximately nine hundred pounds apiece. I saw the poles lifting off the ground about two feet.

Many people, filled with fear, got up, ready to run out of the tent. I thought panic could cause many people to get hurt. The Spirit of God came upon me, and I said, "Please sit back down. I am going to command that wind to stop blowing. It will cease blowing until after the service and give me an opportunity to finish my sermon. Nobody will be hurt." The folks sat down, and I continued with my sermon. Many people were saved that night, and many others were healed.

After the service was over and the people had all gone home, the wind broke loose in all its fury, and the wind again blew at eighty miles an hour. We fought to hold the tent together, but I could see that we were going to lose it, so I ordered that the tent be let down to the ground. We folded all the chairs and laid them on the ground. We laid gunny sacks over the piano and the corners of the platform, so that the tent would not be torn. With the tent flat on the ground, we went to sleep. I was staying in the motel across the street from the New Mexico Fairgrounds, where the tent was pitched.

The next day we put the tent back in the air, and the thousands of people who came to church that night did not know that we had taken the tent down during the night. So many people were coming to the services that we borrowed chairs from every funeral home in town, and we asked people to bring their own chairs with them.

Some people estimated that upwards of ten thousand people attended the meetings because, with all the extra chairs filled, many people still had to stand around the outside of the tent. I figured that it was safe to say that five thousand were in attendance each night.

In stilling the terrible wind while the service was in progress, I believe that God kept many people from getting hurt, for the wind was rushing down from the top of the mountains to the north of town and hitting the tent with full force. I had suffered through a big tent of mine blowing down seven times over the years, so I had to have known that it was God who came upon me and told the folks to sit back down and enjoy the service.

- 143 -

"I Saw One Hundred and Fifty-three People Lying on the Ground"

One time I was conducting a revival meeting in Brother Heflin, Sr.'s tent in Richmond, Virginia. A terrible storm hit the tent in the middle of the service. I had seen my tent blown down seven times, so I told Brother Heflin, "Let's dismiss the people, let them go home, and we'll take the tent down, for this is a powerful storm."

Brother Heflin said, "No, I have been praying for a large crowd to attend our revival, and we have the largest attendance tonight that we have ever had; and we are not going to send them home."

Soon I went back to Brother Heflin, saying, "Please send the people home, for I have just had a vision of one hundred and fifty-three people lying on the ground here."

He answered, "No, we are not going to close this meeting. This is the greatest meeting that we have had, and God is not going to let the tent blow down. You go ahead and preach."

I answered, "I am preaching entirely on your faith, for I have had this strong vision of one hundred and fifty-three people lying on the ground in puddles of water."

I preached, and God gave us a wonderful service. The ground under the tent was soaking wet with big puddles of water everywhere, but the storm had passed by safely. The Holy Ghost fell upon the altar service, and people were slain in the Spirit everywhere. They were lying on the ground, many half in and half out of puddles of water. Many were receiving the baptism of the Holy Ghost, and many were being healed by the power of God, and a great many had just been converted, and were lying in the presence of the Lord.

God told me to count the people lying on the ground. I did, and there were one hundred and fifty-three people lying there, exactly as I had seen in the vision. I had thought that they must be lying on the ground because the tent had blown down, and they were hurt, but instead they were lying there under the power of the Precious Holy Spirit in complete victory.

I was certainly thankful that Brother Heflin, Sr. had

not listened to me, but had operated on his own faith, which was far greater than mine at the time.

- 144 -

They Gave Me a New Packard Automobile

In my revival in Plainview, Texas, a terrible storm hit the tent on the last Saturday night after the service. We had to take the tent down, and most people had already gone home. I stood in water above my knees as we were lowering the tent, and every time the lightning flashed, my legs would shake uncontrollably, hitting one another at the knees. I realized that I could easily be electrocuted, but I was trying to protect the tent as well as I could. It was after 1:00 A.M., when we just left the tent on the ground and went to bed.

The next day was Sunday, and we were supposed to close with a big service. We did not know what to do. People had to attend the Sunday morning services of the five churches which were sponsoring the tent meeting, and we knew that there would not be enough time to put the tent back up for Sunday night. Someone came up with the idea of renting the city auditorium for Sunday night. So we did.

I thought that since there had been no time to advertise the Sunday auditorium meeting, there probably would be a small crowd, but I was pleasantly surprised to see that the auditorium was completely packed out. Even the balcony was filled, and people were standing.

During the song service, I looked at three sponsoring preachers on the platform who all had new Packard automobiles. I sat on the platform and, in my heart, I said, "Dear Lord, there is pastor Louie Shultz who has a new Packard. There is Pastor W. Hathcock who has a new Packard, and there is Pastor Walter Lane leading the song service who has a new Packard, and I don't even have a bicycle."

I never told any human being that I wanted a car. But just then Pastor Walter Lane, leading the song service said, "God just spoke to me, saying, 'Pastor Louie Shultz has a new Packard automobile, Pastor W. Hathcock has a new Packard. I have a new Packard, but Brother Ward doesn't even have a bicycle.' I think that we should take up an offering and buy him a new Packard, also."

A man jumped up, shouting, "I will give the first hundred dollars." In a few minutes the money was given to buy me a new Packard, and the next day they brought a new Packard automobile to me as a gift from the people of Plainview, Texas.

- 145 -

A Boy, Hit by a Tent Pole, Was Thought to be Killed

When we were taking the tent down after the last service in Tucson, Arizona, we were lowering the seven center poles to the ground. As I have said elsewhere, these center poles were thirty-five feet tall and weighed about nine hundred pounds a piece. When we came to the last pole, a boy began to play in the center of the tent area. I asked, "Fathers, please keep your sons by you and don't let any boy play around where we are taking this pole down."

A man spoke up saying, "I want my boy near me. I want to be able to see where he is. He will be all right."

Just then the center pole got away from the men and fell to the ground, hitting the boy. It sounded like thunder; the crack of the pole hitting the boy was so loud.

All the men began to scream and run to the boy, trying to help. They lifted the pole off the boy. The father cried for me to come pray for his son. He said, "I can find no sign of life in him."

I went down, and I could find no pulse, no sign of breathing, and I began to pray, "Dear God, I command this boy to come to life, in the Name of Jesus. We are not going to allow the devil to ruin this great revival by killing this boy on the last night of the meetings. This is God's hour for complete victory."

The boy opened his eyes and looked at me. I asked, "Do you hurt anywhere?"

He replied, "No, I don't hurt any place."

I told his father, "There is a large hospital next door. Go, have your boy's body x-rayed from head to toe. We will pay for the x-rays. We cannot leave town until we know absolutely about your son. I will stay right here until you get back and tell me what the doctors say."

He was gone at least two hours, and then I saw the father and the son walking across the field to us. The father said, "They have x-rayed my son from top to bottom. He has absolutely no broken bones. He is in no pain whatsoever. The doctors say that we can go home. My boy is all right."

We all gathered in a circle and thanked God that we could go home rejoicing, knowing that God had let our revival meeting end in victory.

- 146 -

The Perfume of Her Desire Followed Her

In 1956 our family moved to Richmond, Virginia, to pastor a church that we founded called The Peoples Church. Brother Heflin, Sr. asked his daughter Ruth to come over and play the organ for us. She played the organ for several years until God called her to do missionary work.

In 1964, Sister Ruth left with her father and mother to conduct revivals in India, where they preached to upwards of thirty thousand people. When they stopped in Paris, France, Ruth went to a store and saw some French perfume. She had no money, but she prayed, "Oh, Lord, I would love to have some of that special French perfume." She had to leave the country with her parents enroute to India, and because she had no money, she had to leave France without her favorite perfume.

Soon after they arrived in India, Sister Ruth was sitting on a veranda, when an automobile drove up and two French ladies asked, "Do you mind if we park our car and eat our lunch in the shade of that big tree?"

Ruth answered, "It is not my house, but please help yourselves."

After lunch the women, who were French tourists, said, "For your kindness, we would like you to have this." And each woman brought out a bottle of Ruth's favorite French perfume and gave it to her.

Sister Ruth had prayed for some of that special perfume in France, and God had sent these two French women as emissaries to India, in order to bring that perfume all the way to India for His chosen servant. And it did not cost Sister Ruth a penny either.

- 147 -

Woman Who Did Not Want to Come to the Tent

In my revival on the fairgrounds in Albuquerque, New Mexico, a woman sent word to me to please come to her house and pray for her healing. I went over to her home and was just starting to pray for her, when God told me, "The reason that this woman asked you to come to her house and pray is that her church does not believe in your healing campaigns, and she does not want anyone to see her at your services. Ask her to come to the tent and be healed."

So I told her what God had just told me, and she admitted that it was certainly the truth. She had been confined to a wheelchair for eighteen years, and she really needed healing, but I said, "I am not going to pray for you in your home. However, if you will be in the big tent on the fairgrounds Sunday afternoon at 3:00 P.M., God will heal you."

I had forgotten about the lady, but as I stood up to preach Sunday afternoon, the woman's husband wheeled her to the front of the pulpit. She stated, "You said that if I would be here this afternoon, I would be healed."

I stepped down from the platform and prayed for her. I affirmed, "Your husband has wheeled you up here, now you get out of that chair and push the chair around this tent."

She got out of the chair and started pushing it. Her husband followed right behind her so that if she fell, he could catch her.

I shouted, "Sister, tell your husband to sit down."

She turned and said, "Husband, sit down. God is doing this work, and I am not going to fall down." She walked all over that big tent that was bigger than a football field.

She had been in a wheelchair eighteen long years, and she was going to enjoy the rest of her life, healed by the power of God. Even though her church did not believe in healing and said that it could not be done, she knew that it had been done by the power of God.

I reiterate, I am no healer. I had nothing to do with the miracle. Only God can heal and deliver.

- 148 -

Sixty-three Doctors Said It Was Impossible

Over the years, I have held something like thirty-five revivals at the Cornerstone Church in Richlands, Virginia. In my first revival there, a blind woman was healed. She went home, where they were watching Dr. Kissinger on television. She said, "So that is what Dr. Kissinger looks like." Her family was astonished, when they determined that she really could see.

The lady told her doctor at the University of Virginia Hospital that she was healed and could see. He said that it was impossible for her to see. She proved to him that she could see. He called in a consultation of doctors. In due time, sixty-three doctors working with the hospital said that according to her records, it was impossible for her to see.

Once her doctor called in a woman doctor, who said that it was impossible for her to see. The woman doctor asked the lady, "What am I doing that is unusual?"

The lady answered, "You just took off your shoes

and are standing there by the window in your stocking feet."

The woman doctor then asked her to describe what was happening across the street.

The lady answered, "That man carrying groceries down the street just went up the steps and entered that house."

In spite of the sixty-three doctors saying, "According to your records, you cannot see," she continued to walk to the church and home again by herself and attend the revival services. She told us often what she had seen on television that day.

God is not limited by what doctors say. He can still work His miracles.

- 149 -

The Preacher Said, "God Does Not Heal Today"

In that same revival at the Cornerstone Church in Richlands, Virginia, a three-and-a-half-year-old boy who had never been able to stand or walk was healed and began to walk perfectly. But the father went to a church that did not believe that God healed the sick.

Three or four times a week the man's pastor would come over and say, "God does not heal the sick today, so that had to be the devil that healed your son." The pastor kept trying to get the father to say that the devil had healed his boy.

Finally, after three months or more, the father wilted and said to the preacher, "You must be right. You know so much about the Bible; it was not God who healed my boy. As you say, the devil healed my boy." Instantly his son, who had been walking beautifully for more than three months, had a relapse, sank back into the place where he could no longer walk, and became the same crippled boy that he was originally.

There are some people who would rather believe their church doctrine than believe God.

- 150 -

God Calls As a Man Is About to Commit Suicide

One day I was preaching in our church in Washington, D.C. In the middle of my sermon, I had a vision. I saw a man running toward the Potomac River to hurl himself into the waters and commit suicide. I cried out, "JESUS, save this man, turn him around, cause him to come to this church, and tell us about his conversion."

Then I told the congregation about my vision. I said, "I believe that the man may come here before this service is over and tell us of his experience."

I had just finished my sermon, when a man walked into the church. He stood in the middle of the aisle and asked, "May I say something, please?"

I answered, "Yes."

He said, "Tonight, I gave up on life. I was running toward the Potomac River, about ten or twelve blocks from here. I was going to throw myself in the river and commit suicide, but before I reached the river, I suddenly heard someone shout 'Jesus.' I stopped and looked around to see who shouted. I saw Jesus. He had His hands out toward me, as though He were saying, 'Throw yourself in my arms instead of the river.' He won my heart. I gave my life to Him, and now I am saved.

"As I left the river, I felt a hand on my shoulder, leading me. I was led to this church. I saw that it was open, and I came in. I felt that I must tell you my story."

I answered, "Brother, I am the man who shouted, 'Jesus.' I asked God to save your soul, and God led you here to assure us that He does hear and answer prayer."

- 151 -

Two Water-head Babies in Texas

I held a five-week revival in Pella, Texas. It was like a suburb of Houston. There were three towns together: Pella, Baytown, and Goose Creek. I preached in all three of them. Now, however, I believe that they have all been incorporated into one town – Baytown.

I especially loved my revival in Pella, because there were two brothers who were midgets that had been in the Barnum and Bailey Circus for years. These two brothers played trumpets, and my, how beautifully they played them. I don't think that they missed one night in the five weeks of meetings. I looked forward to seeing and hearing them play every night.

One night people brought two babies who had water-heads to church for healing. Their heads were so big that they had to lie down all the time. Their heads seemed as big as watermelons. I laid my hand gently on each head and prayed God to heal them, and I felt those heads shrink down under my hand. Soon their heads were normal.

When they saw those babies healed, the midget brothers began playing their trumpets in triumph. And I have never forgotten how wonderful it was. From that time, God gave me special faith for babies who had water-head. I have seen probably more than a dozen such babies healed by the power of God.

- 152 -

There Is Over $1,300 Cash in This Building

One night the late Rev. Wallace Heflin, Sr. and I drove quite a ways to a church out in the country to have service. Brother Heflin asked me to take the offering. Since we had driven possibly eighty or ninety miles to get there, and we had the same amount of miles to return, I felt that we should certainly receive enough money to pay for the gas for the car. But we only got several dollars.

Disappointed, I found myself saying, "There is over thirteen hundred dollars in cash in this building tonight, and yet I cannot get thirteen dollars in the offering." I never heard anything about that episode for fifteen or sixteen years. Then one day I heard Brother Heflin, Sr. preaching, and I heard him tell the story in his sermon.

He said, "One night, Brother Ward and I drove out to this church in the country. When Brother Ward could not get more than a couple of dollars in the offering, he said, 'There is over thirteen hundred dollars in cash in this church tonight, and I cannot get even thirteen dollars in the offering.' "

After church, the deacons met and said, 'We are going to prove that preacher to be a liar. We are going to show him and the whole congregation that there was not $1,300 cash in the church tonight.' So the deacons went to the door and, as the people left, they asked each one how much cash he had on him.

"When the last person left, they found that there had been more than $1,300 in cash on the people that night. Instead of finding the visiting preacher to be a liar, they discovered that he had been speaking under the anointing of the Holy Ghost."

- 153 -

A Demon-possessed Woman Tried to Choke Me

In Bakersfield, California, when I was conducting a revival for my great friend, Rev. Danny Davis, one night a sweet woman came on the platform before the service and began to talk to me. She was so kind and considerate.

All of a sudden her eyes changed. I could see demons looking out of her eyes. Her face became contorted in absolute hate for me. She became like a monster. She leaped for my throat and began choking me. Six men in the church saw what was happening and they rushed to my help. She began throwing those big men around like they were weak little boys.

Finally the six men wrestled her to the floor and were holding her down. By this time I had regained my composure and had begun rebuking the demons, commanding them to come out of her. They did come out, ranting and raving as they left her. The men saw the change in her and returned to their seats.

She sat back on the platform and resumed her conversation with me as though nothing had happened. She was her sweet self again. In a few minutes, she asked me, "Did something strange happen here a few minutes ago?"

- 154 -

"How Many Revivals Have You Held?"

In Tulsa, Oklahoma, while I pastored Bethel Temple, I fasted twenty-one days, praying for God to give us a mighty, old-fashioned revival at the church. One day, a boy named Paul Cain came to see me, saying, "God sent me to Tulsa to hold you a revival."

I asked him how old he was.

He answered, "Seventeen."

I asked him further, "How many revivals have you conducted?"

He answered, "None."

All the clockwork went spinning around in my brain. I asked myself, "How can this seventeen-year-old boy, who has never held a revival in his life, give me the kind of meetings that I am praying God to give us? I have no proof that he could even conduct such a revival." So I told him, "We had better pray about this."

Paul Cain left our church, but he wanted to hold a revival, so he went four or five blocks away and asked another preacher for a meeting. The preacher said, "Yes."

Then I kept hearing of this mighty revival going on at the neighboring church, where they had a harder time getting a crowd than we had. I heard that it was the greatest revival that had come to any of the churches in Tulsa in many years. I heard that ambulances were bringing people from the hospitals, and the people were being healed by the power of God. I heard that this wonderful evangelist was telling people their names and addresses, and many things about their lives. The entire city of Tulsa was agog with spiritual excitement. I cried to God, "That is the kind of revival that I want at our church."

The revival continued at our neighbor church. I think that it was going into the seventh week. I could stand it no longer. I said, "I must go to that church. Things are really happening there. I want to see who that evangelist is."

When I reached the church, there was an ambulance unloading a woman on a stretcher. Men were carrying her inside. The church was packed out. I could not get into the building.

I thought, "Why, this church never had a crowd like this before." I walked around among the crowd filling the sidewalks and street outside the church, wishing that I could get in and see what was happening.

Suddenly, a deacon of the church saw me and recognized me as the neighboring preacher up the street. He said, "Dr. Ward, every seat in the house is filled, but I will take you in and seat you next to the evangelist on the platform."

I answered, "Wonderful, let's go."

He took me in a side door, escorted me to the platform, and sat me next to the evangelist. Then the evangelist turned around to greet me and, lo and behold, it was the seventeen-year-old boy, who had wanted to bring this wonderful revival to our church, but I had been too stupid and stuffy to allow him to do so. If I could have kicked myself, I would have done it, right there on the platform.

I watched as God used that seventeen-year-old Paul Cain. He would tell people about their sickness, what their doctor's name was and what the doctor had told them that very morning.

The whole city of Tulsa, Oklahoma, was turned upside down for God, and all that I could think of was that I had fasted twenty-one days for a revival to break out, and I could have had this mighty revival in our church. God had sent Paul Cain from Dallas, Texas, to Tulsa, Oklahoma, to me, but I was too "hotsy-totsy, tootsie-wootsy" to have a young boy who had never held a revival before.

But, believe me, I learned my lesson. Now I know that it is God who gives the revival, and the Babe who was born in a barn can use anybody, who will let Him move. For "God moves in mysterious ways, His wonders to perform."

- 155 -

Three Short Straws

In the Cave of Adullam I see a prophetic picture; for David, who was going to be King, had a prophet and a priest traveling with him. God brought a prophet named Gad to stand by David's left side and a priest named Abiathar to stand by his right side.

The prophet was to direct his goings, and the priest was to bless and anoint him on his travels. But we do not need to have a local prophet and priest travel with us now, because we have all three offices of Christ: the Prophet, Priest and King functioning inside of us.

But when I was only seventeen, I was ignorant of these things. I wanted to know whether I was to attend a Bible college in Missouri or a Bible college in Rhode Island. So I asked my mother to make three long straws and three short straws and hold them so that I could not tell which were long and which were short. Since I was young and meant well, God put up with me. Immediately I drew the three short straws without a miss, and attended Zion Bible College in East Providence, Rhode Island. I have been thankful all these years because I did attend there, for they were on fire for God, and they got me on fire for the Lord, too.

I was later told that if you are on fire for God you can go anywhere in America and preach. So I feel that this helped me to preach in every state in the United States, in eighty-eight nations of the world, and in nearly every big city on Earth. I later went to seven colleges and universities, receiving fourteen years of higher education, but I always feel that it was my first three years in Zion Bible Institute in East Providence, Rhode Island, which gave me the foundation for my ministry. God bless the memory of Rev. Christine A. Gibson who was Founder and President of that school.

But today, I repeat, we do not need to draw straws to find the will of God, because we have the office of the prophet, priest and king residing inside of us, and there is a small voice of the prophet within us, saying, "This is the way, walk ye in it," there is the voice of the priest, saying, "Be blessed as you travel," and the voice of the king, saying, "Realize who you are as you journey on your way."

- 156 -

Three Thousand Dollars, a Thousand at a Time

I believe that it was 1957, and I was buying the church building on Hull Street in Richmond, Virginia. I needed $9,000 to pay on the building. I had fasted fifty-seven days on liquids, asking God for the $9,000. I told the Lord, if He would send me $3,000 immediately, I could trust Him for the other $6,000 to come in shortly.

As I was preaching, I saw a woman who seemed to need a new dress. I walked over in front of her and prayed in my heart (not out loud), "Dear Lord, send this dear lady two new dresses." The Lord answered me, "This is the woman who is going to give you the three thousand dollars that you want now." I was flabbergasted, because I had always considered that lady as one of the poorest persons in the church.

After service she said, "Brother Ward, meet me

down at Franklin Federal Savings tomorrow morning at ten o'clock. I want to give you one thousand dollars." She gave me the thousand, and I thanked her.

I went home and told my wife. "She gave me a thousand, but tomorrow morning she will call me to meet her at the savings and loan again, for God told me that she is going to give me three thousand dollars." Of course, I did not tell anyone else about the $3,000, and certainly not the lady who was going to give it.

The next morning, she called me and said, "Brother Ward, meet me at Franklin Savings at ten o'clock. I want to give you another $1,000." I met her, and she handed me the second $1,000.

I went home and told my wife, "Tomorrow morning, she will call me again and give me the third $1,000."

The following morning, she called once again, saying, "Brother Ward, meet me at Franklin Federal Savings, I want to give you another thousand dollars." I met her and she handed me the third thousand.

I went home and told the Lord, "Since You have given me this three thousand dollars from a woman who I always considered the poorest person in the church, I can trust you for the other six thousand dollars easily." The $6,000 came in shortly, like in a week or so.

About two weeks later, the sister who had given me the $3,000, came to me saying, "Brother Ward, a wonderful thing has happened. God has just given me two new dresses." I had not told her or anyone else that I had prayed for her to get two new dresses, but God remembers every little detail of our prayers, and He always answers.

- 157 -

Existing in a Totally Dark Room

In Charlotte, North Carolina, I was asked to pray for a woman in the insane asylum. They warned me not to lift a shade or light a match, because she had to live in total darkness. They informed me that tape had been put around the shades on the windows, so that not one little ray of light could penetrate her room.

When I entered the room, I had to stand still for some time until my eyes got adjusted to the darkness. Then I finally made out the form of a woman, sitting on the side of the bed. She had to sit in that total darkness, day and night. She could not stand for any small ray of light to enter her life.

She told me that she could not forgive herself for something that she had done. I told her that God's forgiveness is unconditional, even though people want to earn God's forgiveness by punishing themselves. This only ends in self-rejection and life-rejection, but that all we can do is ask for forgiveness and then RECEIVE God's forgiveness. God's love is rooted in His forgiveness, and when He so gladly forgives us, He places our sins in the Sea of His Forgetfulness, never to remember them again. I said, "God has forgiven you and has forgotten your sin, so now forgive yourself and forget your sin, also."

I wish that I could tell you that I know unequivocally that the woman was delivered, but the authorities saw to it that I left the woman in the same physical darkness in which I found her. However, I have a ray of hope where the woman is concerned, because she began to pray with me and call on God. Her attitude changed. I felt that she was accepting God's forgiveness. She told me that when I returned, I would find the shades up and sunlight in her room. However, I was never able to return, because my revival meeting ended, and I left town.

I use this woman's story to teach you not only God's forgiveness, but God's method of deliverance, that if you are going to be healed, you have to TAKE the healing. The last invitation in Revelation reads, *"Come TAKE the water of life freely."* If you get anything from God, you have to TAKE it, because He has already given it to you. So people who get their healing are people who TAKE it. *"And from the days of John the Baptist until now the kingdom of Heaven suffereth violence, and the violent TAKE* (My emphasis) *it by force"* (Matthew 11:12).

Since this woman was in an insane asylum, I figured that her mind was not well, so I TOOK her healing for her. As I said, I never heard anything else about her, but I have always felt in my spirit that she was healed, because I took her healing, and God is so merciful and kind, and He is a Healer.

- 158 -

I Received a Strange, Wonderful Letter

I received a letter from Lori Ann Green, dated June 10, 1994, stating that she had heard me preach at the Calvary Pentecostal Camp in Ashland, Virginia in 1989. At the close of the service, I laid hands on her. Let me read what she said happened:

"When I came to you for prayer, you laid hands on my head and stated that it (the prayer) was not for me, but rather for someone that I knew. Needless to say, I was a bit baffled but trusted God nonetheless.

"When I returned to New York, I found out that my second oldest sister, Christine, was in Ashland, Virginia, the very night that you laid hands on me. As a matter of fact, she was on a 'gambling bus' and was about to get into a fight with someone who had a knife. I believe in my spirit and with my heart that the Lord spared my sister's life. I have shared this testimony with my family and many other people.

"God bless you for hearkening unto the voice of the Lord."

Isn't it wonderful that God knows all things? He realized that Lori Ann Green's sister needed prayer more, at that very moment, than she did, and He directed me to pray for the other party rather than the one who came up for prayer.

- 159 -

"Put Your Husband's Shoes Under Your Bed"

A lady stopped me on the campgrounds and thanked me for praying that her husband would come home. She said, "I told you several years ago that my husband had left home and was living with another woman. I told you that I could not live without him and that I also needed him to help pay the bills. I asked you what I should do. You told me to place a pair of my husband's shoes under my bed, and that he would soon be home to fill those shoes."

When she told me that, I laughed out loud. I thought that it was so funny. I never remembered telling her that, so I asked, "Are you sure that I told you to do that?"

She replied in the affirmative, and said, "Yes, I placed a pair of my husband's shoes under my bed, and in two or three days he came back home. That has been several years now. He is still home, and we are both happy again."

I have laughed over that story many times. At first, I did not think that I said it, but then I remembered saying it.

- 160 -

Walking Against the Traffic

While I was talking on the Grundy, Virginia, television station, I suddenly had a vision, and said, "I see a woman who is about to be killed. Let us stop and pray for her."

A man told us the next night that a lady was walking down the middle of the highway against the oncoming traffic. He stopped and picked her up. It was his neighbor's wife. He took her to her home. Her husband said that it was the medicine that her doctor had given her that caused her to act erratically, and he profusely thanked the man for his kindness in bringing her home.

- 161 -

A Man Lay in a Coma Twenty-Eight Days

A man was in an accident and lay in a coma at the hospital for twenty-eight days. He could not walk. He was brought to the campmeeting where I was praying for the sick. God instantly healed him, and he began to walk beautifully. He was totally healed in every respect.

- 162 -

I Have Never Been Out of My House in Nine Years

I was on the radio in Richmond, Virginia, and a lady called me to come pray for her. She said, "I have agoraphobia. I have not been out of my house in nine years, not even on the front or back porches."

I said, "Put your coat on; we are going for a walk."

We walked for forty-five minutes. Then I told her, "I want you to walk outside your home for at least thirty minutes every day."

She called me a year later, saying, "I have walked my thirty minutes outside my house for one solid year, and I know that I am healed now."

- 163 -

The Prophetic Gift

When I had the blood clot in my left leg, some people were telling me, "You probably will never walk again." Just then, the doorbell rang. It was the mailman. He gave my wife the pair of shoes Rev. Danny Davis ordered for me before he left town.

It was a prophetic act by Brother Davis. My wife brought the shoes into my bedroom and shouted, as she put the shoes on, and danced around the room in them, "You will walk again, or God would not have told Danny Davis to buy you some shoes."

- 164 -

A Tankful of Blessing

While I was away holding a revival, it turned very cold at home, and soon the fuel tank was empty. My wife had to carry a five gallon can of oil every night, spilling it all the way from the car to the back of the house. This amount of oil would only keep the furnace going during the night. She was working during the day, and Billy, our youngest son was in school, but they had to come home to a very cold house.

She had to lift the heavy can of oil more than a foot off the ground to pour the oil into the tank. One night, she placed the can on the ground and prayed, "Dear God, PLEASE send me some oil. My hands are frozen, and the smell of oil on my coat makes me cough. In the Name of JESUS, send me some oil."

The next night when she came home to get the oil can, there was an invoice on the front door which read, "275 gallons of oil delivered," signed by Fuel Oils. She looked at the address. It was for 9900 Duryea Drive, but our address was 9900 Oldfield Drive.

The next morning my wife called the oil company and asked for the manager. After a rather long wait, the manager came to the phone, and asked, "How may I help you?"

My wife answered, "You already have helped me." She told him that they had delivered the oil to the wrong house and that they should send oil to the neighbors across the street so that they would not run out of oil. If they would wait a few days until I got home from my revival, I would pay for the oil that they had sent us by "MISTAKE."

God had caused a company to make an honest mistake so that my wife would not have to carry oil again and, to this day, she never has.

- 165 -

The Wheel Bounced Right over My Car

In 1935, in Connecticut, on a four-lane highway, a wheel came off the left front of a car that was speeding toward me. The wheel cut across the four lanes of highway and was approaching my car. I only had time to cry out in prayer, "JESUS." The wheel bounced right over my car and went out into a field. It did not hurt anyone.

- 166 -

Mother, You Are So Much Taller

In Roanoke, Virginia, a woman who was terribly hump-backed, was healed. I told her that her three daughters were watching television in the front room of their house, and when she opened the front door, her children were going to turn and cry, "Mother, what happened? You are so much taller!"

The next night, she told me that was exactly what happened. The girls had never seen their mother that tall and straight before.

- 167 -

In the Name Of Jesus, I Create

On one of my visits to Heaven, I watched the Lord create a new universe. Jesus turned and said to me, "I have made you a little creator. The only difference in the way that I create and the way that you create is that you create IN MY NAME." He continued, "As I send you back to Earth, you can create a better life for your family."

One of our children called on the phone and needed money. I prayed, "Dear Lord, I create a better life for her, using your name." My daughter and her girlfriend became real estate brokers. They got their own company, and the next time my daughter needed money, I prayed, "I command her to sell three houses this week, in the name of Jesus." She sold the three houses within a week, and she is living better.

One day she called and said, "I have lost my very important book, and I cannot find it anywhere. It has all the names and addresses of those who want to buy or sell a house." My wife and I joined hands and prayed for an angel to place that book right where she could find it easily.

While we were still praying, she called back, saying, "The book was right on the sofa, where I could not miss it. I had looked there a hundred times, and it was not there; but when I hung up the phone, I walked right to it."

She had called back while we were still praying, thanking God for answering prayer.

- 168 -

I Missed the Number by One

From the very beginning of my revivals, God would give me the number of the people to be saved, and that many would always respond. I was so sure that God had spoken to me that anytime I missed the number, I would say to the people in attendance, "I will never leave this place until that person comes to God."

In Seattle, Washington, we had five churches cooperating in the meeting, and one night I missed the number by one. I said, "I will never leave the tent until that person that God is dealing with comes to Him," and I meant it.

At one-thirty in the morning a sailor boy came back to the tent and was gloriously converted. He gave a letter to one of the cooperating pastors in which he said, "Tomorrow, I leave for the War Zone. If you hear that I have been killed, please give this letter to Brother Ward."

Three weeks later news reached the pastor that the boy had been killed in action, and the pastor sent me the letter to be opened. The letter read, "Dear Brother Ward, I want to thank you so very much for waiting at the tent until one-thirty in the morning for me to return to the tent and be saved. When you read this, I will be in Heaven instead of Hell, because you cared enough to wait for me."

- 169 -

I Missed the Number by Two

One night in Tucson, Arizona, in my big tent, the number God gave me to be saved was something like 276, and I missed it by two. I said to the people there that night, "I will never leave this tent until the other two people that God is dealing with come to Him."

My assistant, Rev. R.L. Franks of Albuquerque, New Mexico, said to me, "If you are going to stay all night in the tent, I am going to stay with you." So the two of us stayed at the altar all night praying.

About seven-thirty in the morning, a car drove up to the tent and a man got out of the car. He said, "My wife and I are looking for the preacher."

I answered, "You have found him."

He replied, "We left home yesterday, about two hundred and fifty miles across the desert, coming to the tent in order to get saved. We would have been here for the service last night, but we had a flat tire and had to wait in the car all night until someone came along that could fix it for us."

I answered, "God told us you were coming to get saved, and we have waited right here at the altar all night for you. Now come in, and we will lead you to Christ. You will never be the same again." The man and his wife both went forward to the altar and God gloriously saved them.

- 170 -

$50,000 and $300,000

A man came to one of my revivals in Richlands, Virginia. I called him to the front of the church, and said, "You must have a large sum of money this year. I am going to give you the first $1 on it." He pinned the $1 in the front of his Bible. He needed $50,000.

When the $50,000 came in answer to prayer, another man came to see him, saying, "I need $300,000. Do you think it might work for me?"

The first man gave him the first dollar on the amount, and the second man pinned the dollar in the front of his Bible. The $300,000 came in answer to prayer to Brother Coy Richardson, too.

After that, every time that I held a revival in

Richlands, and would go by a certain church in town, I would pray, "Dear Lord, let me preach in that church."

One time Brother Tex Sawyers, pastor of the church where I went, said to me, "Rev. David Allen wants you to come and preach for him."

When I arrived at the church to preach, lo and behold, it was the very church where I had been wanting to preach. After the Sunday morning service, the preacher said, "I wanted you to come and preach for me, so that I could tell you this story of the fifty thousand dollars that I got and the three hundred thousand dollars that Brother Coy Richardson received."

I was certainly glad to hear the story, for I had not known that the man I gave the dollar to was a preacher, and I certainly did not know that he was pastor of the church where I had wanted to preach for so long.

- 171 -

Christmas When I Was A Boy

It was Christmas Eve, I was nine years old, and it was about nine o'clock at night. We had nothing in the house to eat but half a box of Puffed Rice with no milk. My mother, sister and I sat in the kitchen with our overcoats on, wrapped in blankets. The only heat in the house was coming from a little gas oven, and we were huddling around it.

Mother said, "Children, it is about time to go to bed, but before we do, let's march around the kitchen, and sing the Doxology." So mother, sister and I began marching around the kitchen, singing:

Praise God from whom all blessings flow.
Praise Him, ye creatures, here below.
Praise Him above, ye heavenly hosts.
Praise Father, Son, and Holy Ghost.
Amen!

I could see angels hanging in the air around us, and see them smiling at us. We were caught up in the Spirit, praising God.

Suddenly, the doorbell rang. I quickly disentangled my hands from my mother's and sister's and ran down the hall and down the stairs to the front door. I knew in my heart that God had come on the scene.

When I flung the door open, two men stood there with a big wooden box. They said, "Ask your mother if we can bring this box into the kitchen."

My mother answered "yes," so the men brought the huge box into the kitchen and pried the lid off. There was more food in that box than I had ever seen anywhere except in a grocery store. The men began filling the cabinets, the counter, the table and every other available space with all kinds of food.

When the men left, I came running back up the stairs crying, "Mamma, let's sing it again. It's working fine." So mother, sister and I began marching around the kitchen singing:

Praise God from whom all blessings flow.
Praise Him, ye creatures, here below.
Praise Him above, ye heavenly hosts.
Praise Father, Son, and Holy Ghost.
Amen!

While we were singing, the doorbell rang again, and I quickly ran down and opened the door. A woman stood there and said, "Merry Christmas. Here is thirty dollars for your mother. An Irish Mail (which was a large, very special wagon) for you, and a present for your sister."

I came running back up stairs crying, "Mamma, let's sing it again, its working fine." So mother, sister and I began marching around the kitchen singing:

Praise God from whom all blessings flow.
Praise Him, ye creatures, here below.
Praise Him above, ye heavenly hosts.
Praise Father, Son, and Holy Ghost.
Amen!

We hardly got any sleep that night for people bringing things all night. Two ladies brought a Christmas tree at eleven o'clock at night and stayed to bedeck it in all of its regal splendor. A man brought a ton of coal at midnight and made us a fire in the furnace.

I was telling my sister the other day that it had been our most wonderful Christmas, and she totally agreed.

When you are at the bottom of life, the Lord can turn things around and put you on the top. So let us all sing praises to our God.

- 172 -

Following in a Great Man's Footsteps

My brother-in-law, the late Rev. Wallace H. Heflin, Sr., always wanted to take Brother Smith Wigglesworth's place, and I think he did; and I always wanted to take Dr. Charles S. Price's place, and in a measure, I think that I did.

I went into A.A. Wilson's church in Kansas City, Missouri. I did not know anyone in his church. Brother Wilson preached, and afterwards I went to the altar, kneeling at a front pew.

Brother Wilson thought that I was a sinner, and he knelt beside me, praying for me. He said, "Oh, God, this man comes to you, asking for forgiveness. Forgive all of his sins right now."

Then God spoke to him, and he said, "Oh, God, I have made a mistake. Why, this is the man that I want to hold me a revival."

He asked me, "Will you come and hold me a revival?"

I was really in awe of Brother Wilson, because he

had the biggest Assembly of God Church in America at that time, and I was only twenty-four years old. I answered, "If you want me, I will be glad to come."

After church, in the course of our conversation, Brother Wilson told me that Charles S. Price had held him the biggest revival that he ever had. He mentioned nine or ten records that he had broken or made in his church. But in the course of our revival, God, through me, broke every record that Dr. Price had made. No glory to me, I was only a twenty-four-year-old boy, but God was allowing me to see that He was honoring my wish to take Dr. Price's place.

In fact, God brought me all the way across America to be there to hear Dr. Price preach his last sermon. It was in the Assemblies of God church in Bakersfield, California, for Rev. C.M. Ward. After the service Dr. Ward asked me to hold him a four-week revival, which I did.

While I was with Dr. Ward, the Assemblies of God asked him to be their national radio speaker. He asked me if he should accept.

I replied, "Just the other day you told me that I was fortunate to live in Washington, D.C., for I could live at the headquarters, from which everything was emanating. And now, you can live in Springfield, Missouri, the headquarters of the Assemblies of God, from which everything in your religious world is emanating."

Yes, God has been so very good to me!

- 173 -

You, Too, Can Have Miracles

By Creation

The greatest thing that ever happened to me in my life was during my approximately twenty visits to Heaven, at a time when I was supposedly dying. On one visit to Heaven, the Lord asked me if I would like to see Him create a new universe, and I quickly said, "Oh yes, Lord."

He took me over to the Balustrades of Heaven. (Mind you that in Heaven you travel with the speed of mind. You just think the thought, and you are there.) Great throngs were already gathered there. Soon Jesus cried with a loud voice, "Let there be light" and light began to burst forth everywhere.

There was scintillant light, flashing light, glittering light, beautiful light, and an angel asked me, "Do you know why the Lord always creates light first?"

I replied, "No, why?"

He answered, "Because light is a sign of wisdom, and Jesus always creates out of His wisdom."

The Lord turned to me and said, "I am sending you back to Earth, but I want you to know that you are a little creator. You can create just as I have created. The only difference in the way you create and I create, is that you always create in My name." He then said, "You can create a better life for your family, when you create in My name."

When I returned to Earth, scientists all over the world began stating that they had found a new universe. It was different than other known universes in that other universes were created out of old, existing materials, while this universe seemed to be created out of new materials. My Richmond, Virginia newspaper printed, "This universe looks like it has come directly from someone's hands."

Not long after that my daughter Gene Ellen who also lives in Virginia called me on the phone to say, "Daddy, I need help."

I remembered what the Lord had told me in Heaven: "You can create a better life for your family, if you create in My name." So I began to say, "I create, in the mighty name of Jesus, a better life for my daughter, Gene Ellen."

Suddenly Gene Ellen and her friend Gloria became enamored of a desire to travel every day to Norfolk, Virginia, to take lessons to become real estate brokers and to open their own real estate agency. They had a combined experience of twenty-five years as agents working for other brokers. They were both single women, and my daughter was supporting her children.

While they were still working in real estate, they would leave home every weekday morning at 6:30 and drive four hours round-trip each day. This continued for four months. Only God gave them the strength to continue.

They passed the rigorous test, and became brokers, and opened their own company. Soon they had one

of the very best real estate companies in
After the first six months of business their accountant said that their achievement had been phenomenal. Both women spoke up in unison and gave all the credit to God. After nearly two years in business the real estate company is nearly out of debt. Both ladies have continued to tell everyone that the company came from God, and they give Him all the glory. It was a real miracle.

Since then, I have told many people all across America, "You can create a better life for your family, if you create in Jesus' name," and I have heard of hundreds of families being blessed by someone creating for them in Jesus' name.

You must know who God is, and you must know who you are in Him. When you know that you are a little creator, and can create mighty things in the name of Jesus, you are on your way to a much better life.

I told one fellow this and he said, "Oh, you are just using the name of Jesus as some magic thing." You can make fun if you want to do so, but I remember what Jesus told me with His own precious lips in Heaven, after I saw Him create a new universe that astounded the whole world.

By Prophecy

Never pray the problem; always prophesy the solution. The miracle is in your mouth. Speak it out.

Prophesy it to happen. Say, "Every bill will be paid by the end of the year." Believe it; accept it; and receive it.

I told one congregation that I was out of debt, and every bill was paid, and a lady cried out, "How about your house; is it paid for?"

That shocked me because I had counted my house payments the same as paying rent. I answered back, "My house is not paid for, but it will be paid in full by Christmas." And it was.

Believe that God is able to do the impossible. In the last nine or ten revivals, I have seen a new part of my ministry unfold. People have come to me saying things like, "Pray for my son. They are going to put him in prison tomorrow." And I have prophesied the release of that son.

I told one weeping mother, "Tomorrow, the judge will say to your son, 'I am going to throw the book at you.' Then he will suddenly change his mind and say, 'Wait a minute. I have decided to give you another chance. You go free. Case dismissed.' " And that was exactly what happened.

Prophesy good things happening to your family, and believe that God is able to bring them to pass.

By Knowing That God Is a Now God

Every miracle must be done in the now. The reason many people do not get their miracle is that they expect God to work Some day in the future. But when God works, He has to work in the now because God lives in a circle, so to speak. His time is always now. Jesus is still the great I AM of the now, and He wants to do a miracle for you NOW.

Notes

Notes

Notes

Other Current Books by Dr. William A. Ward

GOD CAN TURN THINGS AROUND
(An Evangelist looks at the book of John)
$10.00 paperback, $15 Cloth bound

ON THE EDGE OF TIME
(An Evangelist looks at the book of Revelation)
$10.00 Paperback $15.00 Cloth bound

GET OFF THE ASH HEAP
(An Evangelist looks at the book of Job)
$7.00 Paperback only

CHRISTIAN CYBERNETICS
(An Evangelist looks at God's Guidance System)
$7.00 Paperback only

Order from:

William A. Ward
9900 Oldfield Drive
Richmond, Virginia 23235-1810

Ministry address:

Dr. William A. Ward
9900 Oldfield Drive
Richmond, VA 23235